THE NESTING SEASON

The Bird Photographs of
Frederick Kent Truslow

THE NESTING SEASON

The Bird Photographs of
Frederick Kent Truslow

Commentary by Helen G. Cruickshank

Foreword by Olin Sewall Pettingill, Jr.

Afterword by Mildred MacCutcheon Truslow

A Studio Book
The Viking Press
New York

Captions to photographs appearing on pages 1 through 8:

Page 1: An Arctic tern may have traveled from Antarctic seas to lay these two eggs in this flimsy nest on the rocks of foggy Machias Seal Island, Maine. *Page 2:* On Vingt-et-un Islands, Texas, a great egret displays plumes worn during the nesting season. *Page 4:* Look-alike cedar waxwings share the task of feeding their young at Ithaca, New York. *Page 6:* A black skimmer slices the water of Coot Bay, Florida, before swinging back and scooping up minnows attracted by the disturbance. *Page 8:* Following a successful dive, the osprey holds its catch in curved talons and begins its meal.

Photographs and captions Copyright © Mildred MacCutcheon Truslow and John K. P. Stone, as Executors of the Estate of Frederick Kent Truslow, 1979
Text Copyright © Helen Cruickshank, 1979
All rights reserved
First published in 1979 by The Viking Press/ A Studio Book
625 Madison Avenue, New York, N.Y. 10022
Published simultaneously in Canada by
Penguin Books Canada Limited

Library of Congress Cataloging in Publication Data
Truslow, Frederick Kent, 1902-1978.
    The nesting season.
    (A Studio book)
    Includes index.
    1. Birds—Eggs and nests.   2. Birds—Behavior.
I. Cruickshank, Helen Gere.   II. Title.
QL675.T78   1979   598.2′1′6   79-15277
ISBN 0-670-50606-0

Many of the photographs in this book originally appeared in *National Geographic*, whose cooperation we gratefully appreciate.

The Nesting Season was conceived and prepared for publication by AG Editions
    Visual Editor: Ann Guilfoyle
    Designer: Al Cetta

Grateful acknowledgment is hereby made to the National Geographic Society for permission to use the following photographs: western grebe (page 68, above) Copyright © 1965 by the National Geographic Society; pileated woodpecker (page 80, below) Copyright © 1964 by the National Geographic Society.

Printed and bound in the United States of America

Set in CRT Palatino

Acknowledgments

Special thanks to all those whose contributions of time and skill made possible the photographic career of Frederick Kent Truslow.

To Dr. Melville B. Grosvenor, who, as editor and publisher of *National Geographic* magazine, was the first to publish many of these pictures.

To Frederick G. Vosburgh for his great help and encouragement over the years.

To "Buddy" Wisherd for giving so freely of his advice and photographic knowledge.

To Dr. Arthur A. Allen and David G. Allen for many shared experiences in the field.

To Allan Cruickshank, renowned nature photographer and lecturer, for his inspiration to start a new career, and to Helen Cruickshank for her close friendship and her superb text in this book.

To Olin Sewall Pettingill, Jr., well-known ornithologist, for his long-held appreciation of Fred's work expressed so beautifully in his Foreword to this volume.

To Ann Guilfoyle, without whose great help this book would not have been published.

To many friends on the staff of the *National Geographic* magazine, who gave so generously of their encouragement and technical knowledge.

To all the friends in the National Park System, especially the Everglades, for their cooperation and assistance in the field.

Last but not least to our two sons, Kent M. Truslow and Stuart A. Truslow, whose interest and enthusiasm were invaluable.

—MILDRED MACCUTCHEON TRUSLOW

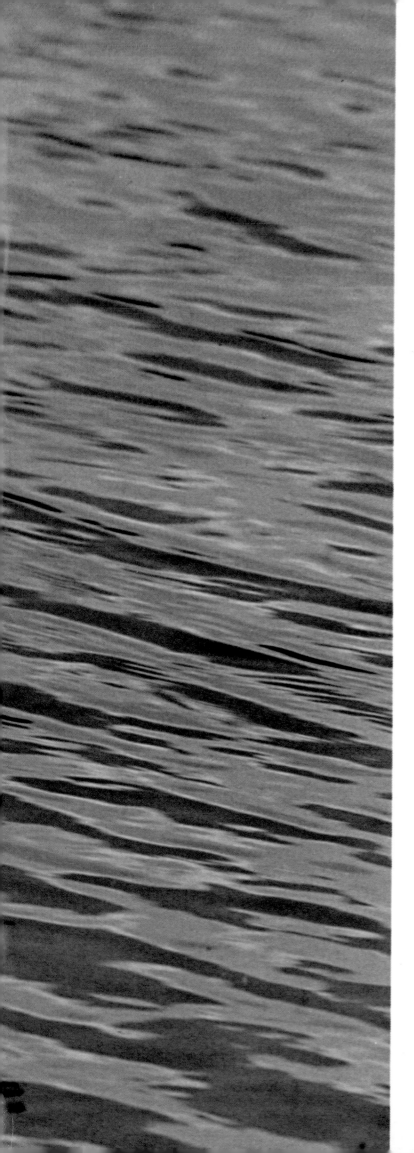

Contents

Foreword by Olin Sewall Pettingill, Jr.   *9*

Commentary by Helen G. Cruickshank   *11*

The Breeding Cycle Begins 13

Claim a Territory, Win a Mate 20

Nest Building 25

The Egg 31

Hatching 37

The Growing Family 41

The Young Birds Fledge 48

Dispersal 54

Index of Latin Names   *59*

The Bird Photographs of

   Frederick Kent Truslow   *63*

Looking Back: An Afterword

   by Mildred MacCutcheon Truslow   *131*

Notes on the Photographs   *135*

Foreword by Olin Sewall Pettingill, Jr.

Readers of the *National Geographic* magazine between 1958 and 1970 know the name of Frederick Kent Truslow for his superb photographs, which illustrated a dozen or more articles about birds. Ornithologists and bird-watchers know the name, too, for his are some of the most remarkable photographs of birds ever taken. The story of the man and his ultimate achievements with the camera bears telling.

Although greatly interested in birds as a youth, Fred Truslow chose industry for a career, eventually becoming a manufacturing executive in New York City. At the early age of fifty-three he retired, anxious to be free of his incumbent responsibilities and pressures. How he would henceforth channel his energies he had given only passing thought until his wife, Mildred, an artist, suggested that he take up photography, specifically the photography of birds, since they continued to interest him as much as ever. On a trip to Florida with camera at hand he launched what would prove to be a second career.

Despite inadequate equipment, Fred's photographs of herons, egrets, ibises, and other Florida birds, obtained by endless patience, were of high enough quality to impress experts at the *National Geographic.* With their aid in acquiring the best of equipment and his consequent experience in using it, his work was soon embellishing the pages of the magazine. In due time, more of Fred's photographs graced the pages of *Audubon,* the magazine of the National Audubon Society, and *The Living Bird,* the annual journal of the Cornell Laboratory of Ornithology.

Thanks to recent advances in developing more sophisticated camera equipment, which is now readily available to photographers, amateurs as well as professionals, excellent photographs are commonplace these days. Even so, the Truslow bird photographs stand out among them for what they show and document.

Fred was an in-depth photographer. Rather than striving to photograph as many different bird species as possible in a given season, he tended to concentrate on one species at a time, usually a nesting pair. From a nearby blind he spent whole days for days on end. In a sense, he practically lived with the birds. At the end of each day he summarized his observations meticulously and copiously in a field notebook. The result of his perseverance—besides the physical endurance involved—was a thorough record, useful to ornithologists in multitudinous ways, often revealing behaviors heretofore unknown, in some cases not even imagined. His unforgettable shots of a pileated woodpecker removing eggs from its nest are a notable example.

Fred was also a purist. Working with birds under control never appealed to him. He preferred to photograph birds at the nest, always careful not to disturb them while setting up his blind, or when entering or leaving it. There was no tampering with the nest site beyond clearing away obstacles in the foreground, no "prettying up" the nest, no coercing the occupant birds to perform. Photographing the natural course of behavior in a natural setting was his goal.

We have in this handsome volume some of Fred's finest photographs, especially selected from his vast collection to illustrate the nesting season. Helen Gere Cruickshank, long an admirer of Fred's work and herself a skilled bird photographer as well as a gifted writer, prepared the captions based on Fred's field notes. In addition, Mrs. Cruickshank wrote the text, providing us with a unifying background for further elucidation of the nesting season.

To Frederick Kent Truslow and his superlative achievements with the camera, this volume is an everlasting memorial.

Commentary by Helen G. Cruickshank

The Breeding Cycle Begins

There is a mysterious time clock in animals that triggers a fantastic variety of responses which have been perfected through countless generations to insure the successful reproduction of each species. One of the most spectacular of these responses is the migration of birds along traditional routes. Built into each bird is the ability to find its way across half the world and more from its wintering place to the area where its ancestors have bred for innumerable centuries.

Guided by instinct, billions of them stream over the pathless oceans and up river valleys, spill through mountain gaps, and sail along ridges to the forests, marshes, fields, or tundra where they will raise their young, each species dropping out as it arrives at its preferred habitat. Countless numbers of birds, particularly ducks and shorebirds, continue on to the far north and even beyond the Arctic Circle. Barring catastrophes caused by abnormal weather conditions and other unusual factors, they arrive at each break in their journey when food is available and reach their destination when snow and ice have receded, leaving the land open for nesting, and when the time for living there is best.

Any mass movement of animals between two areas is a migration. Some insects, fish, and mammals make spectacular annual journeys, but in the popular mind migration means first of all the passage of birds. The arrival of birds at their nesting ground has been associated with the coming of spring since the Pleistocene Era. At one time the movements of nomadic tribes were governed largely by the appearance and disappearance of birds, while the ancient Persians named the months of their calendar year for the birds that were dominant at each period. The Book of Exodus (16:13) may contain the first written reference to the migration of birds, and Homer in the *Iliad* sang of the migrating cranes (probably *Megalornis grus*):

As when the cranes,
Flying the wintry storms, send forth on high
Their dissonant clamors, while o'er the ocean stream
They steer their course.

Many of the ancient explanations for the seasonal appearance and disappearance of birds amuse us today, but it must be remembered that most people lived out their entire lives within a very restricted area and had little conception of the world beyond their limited horizons. As late as 1492 Columbus noted land birds traveling in a southwest direction and ordered a change of course to follow them, not realizing that the birds were simply passing over the ocean on their way to South America. As a result of his misunderstanding, he discovered San Salvador instead of the North American continent, from which the birds were migrating.

Well into the eighteenth century, many naturalists thought that swallows, swifts, and other small birds plunged into mud for the winter and hibernated there as toads do. Others thought they hibernated in caves and rock crevices. Modern ornithologists dismissed this ridiculous theory until December 1946, when Dr. Edmund C. Jaeger found a poor-will hibernating in the crevice of a canyon in southeast California. In a few weeks it awakened to normal life, only to return to the same crevice the following winter. It has been observed that some swifts go into a torpid state for days at a time during cold, rainy weather, though it has not yet been proved that they truly hibernate. One ancient theory held that the transmutation of species explained the mystery of seasonal changes in bird populations. Aristotle wrote that European robins changed in summer into European redstarts, and for countless centuries people believed that goose barnacles changed into barnacle geese when spring arrived. Emperor

Frederick II wrote in 1245 that he greatly doubted this legend, but it continued to find credence until the early nineteenth century. People who accepted the idea that large birds were strong enough to travel to warm climates during the winter imagined that small birds were not and must therefore be transported on the backs of more powerful species. In 1703 a paper published in London described the flight of birds to the moon, a trip, so it claimed, that took sixty days. While making the long flight, the birds hurtled through space at a terrific speed and, since they found no food on the moon, they hibernated until it was time to synchronize their return to earth with the arrival of spring.

The eighteenth-century Philadelphia naturalist William Bartram was the first American to grasp the true meaning of migration. An acute observer, Bartram traveled across more than 30 degrees of latitude, and this range enabled him to understand the significance of the departure of birds that wintered in Florida and their arrival in his home state of Pennsylvania in early spring. Nevertheless, the origin of migration will always be shrouded in mystery. Although we know that certain birds follow routes where they can take advantage of the best air currents to save energy and we suspect that they navigate at least in part by celestial light, we still do not understand the factors that enable each bird to find its way back even to the exact spot where it nested the previous year. We can observe what birds do, and where and when, but the reasons for their behavior can never be completely determined, any more than we can say how the physical rhythm of a human being is set in motion or why our own time clocks operate as they do.

Black-necked stilt (*Himantopus mexicanus*)

Laboratory studies explain certain facets of migration, but no single explanation is possible; there are too many variables. The explanation lying behind bird migration may be as varied as the number of species that engage in annual migrations. For the past several years the movements of birds recorded by radar have revealed some strange and wonderful flights over the Atlantic made by both songbirds and shorebirds. As many as twelve million may take off from Cape Cod in a single autumn night, and most fly without stopping for as long as eighty-six hours over the ocean before making a landfall on the South American coast. Their direction is generally southeast until they near Antigua, where the winds shift direction and the birds swing with them toward the southwest. Soon after leaving the North American coast, most ascend to somewhat more than a mile above the sea; in the region of Bermuda they begin to climb higher until their altitude over Antigua may be as much as twenty-one thousand feet, where the temperature is freezing and the air has half the oxygen present at sea level. Then the birds begin to descend (none has been recorded above 2624 feet over Tobago, for instance) and they continue to lose altitude until they reach the mainland of South America.

Banding records have documented extraordinary migratory flights. An Arctic tern banded on the west coast of Greenland holds the world record so far, established when it was picked up off the southeast coast of Africa more than ten thousand miles from its birthplace. These terns are circumpolar, nesting in suitable places in the higher latitudes all around the northern hemisphere. They are often called birds of the sunlight, for they nest in the north, where summer days are long, and, as the sun moves southward, follow it to the southern hemisphere when days are long there. Many of the terns winter off Africa's Cape of Good Hope and some of them may wander as far as the Antarctic Circle. Then as the sun again turns north, the Arctic terns go with it, moving up the west coast of Africa until they approach Europe, then turn west, some flying north to Greenland, some moving toward Baffinland, perhaps continuing on to nest where they find open land some four hundred and fifty miles from the North Pole, while others swing south toward our northeast coast and drop down on one of several oceanic islands. A typical choice is Matinicus Rock off the coast of Maine, where one of their lively nesting colonies has existed for as long as man has known the area. As the terns hover above their nests, their slim, graceful bodies with long, forked tails give an impression of leashed power almost too great to control. The terns that sweep effortlessly around the Rock make their long flights from ocean to ocean and from hemisphere to hemisphere, living always where the days are longest and the sun is brightest.

Scientists tell us that the breeding cycle of birds is initiated when the increased light and warmth of approaching spring cause the sex organs to swell. These factors may stimulate the development of the gonads in birds wintering north of the equator, but what stimuli trigger the birds wintering in the southern hemisphere, where days are growing shorter and light is decreasing, to set off toward the higher latitudes of the northern hemisphere? It seems that as each new fact is established a new mystery looms ahead.

We can, in any case, understand some advantages of the dangerous journeys birds make. The annual change of diet undoubtedly fosters good health, and the physical challenge of migration weeds out the weak, the sick, and the old. The mixing of individuals from widely separated parts of their habitat contributes vigor to the species. Perhaps the most important advantage of migration, however, is the length of days in the higher latitudes as opposed to the evenly divided day and night of the tropics. Young birds, so vulnerable in their nests, fledge more quickly when fed throughout the extra hours of sunlight.

At some moment on or about March 21, the direct rays of the sun touch briefly on the equator, signaling the beginning of the northern spring. These direct rays continue their slow march northward at about fifteen miles each twenty-four hour-period until the last day of spring, when they actually pour about a fifth more heat on the ice-bound North Pole than on the equator. The coming of spring in the northern hemisphere is the signal to birds that have wintered in Africa, South America, and the innumerable islands, great and small, of the southern seas to surrender their restful lives. The urge to reproduce their kind takes possession of them. They arrow toward the northern hemisphere, following certain flyways over broad geographical areas that each has used generation after generation. Usually the birds make a fairly direct flight, sweeping northward in a wide front from their wintering grounds to the areas where suitable nesting places await them. As the birds move from one part of the world to another, there is scarcely a rock in the loneliest ocean, the most remote piece of open land in the polar regions, or the smallest desert oasis that is not, at some time, visited by some bird. Wherever food is available, on land or sea, some species has adapted to take advantage of it. Moreover, each species knows instinctively the direction its flight should take it. The golden plover (*Pluvialis apricaria*) that winters in Africa flies toward northern Europe while the American golden plover (*Pluvialis dominica*) leaves South America, aiming directly toward the American arctic to nest. Though the two golden plovers are difficult to separate in the field, neither species is confused about its destination.

If you travel by automobile from the Atlantic Ocean westward across Texas when barn swallows are migrating north, you will be able to see these swallows for more than two thousand miles, so wide is their migrating path and so great is their number. Moving north as if pulled by invisible threads, the swallows swerve to right and left catching insects as they travel, but they always keep to that boreal direction. Other species may travel in compact flocks. Occasionally a great flock of bobolinks that has wintered in Argentina will settle in a spacious orange grove in Florida, where they appear weary after their crossing of the Gulf of Mexico, but usually the next morning they are all gone, irresistibly drawn toward their nesting meadows farther north.

The metabolism of birds is so rapid that a regular intake of food is essential. They are able to store up a certain amount of fat before migration begins, but few except shorebirds can make their long journeys without stopping to eat along the way. When they have met strong headwinds I have seen exhausted migrants drop onto the parade ground at Fort Jefferson on the Dry Tortugas, where so little food is available that they die if they lack the strength to resume quickly their flight to the mainland, still more than a hundred miles away.

Great Egrets (*Casmerodius albus*) and Snowy Egrets (*Egretta thula*)

Many birds that winter in Africa must cross the dangerous Sahara on their migration to nesting places in Europe and Asia. Then as they approach the Mediterranean they swing into three loosely formed prongs. Birds going toward Western Europe make the crossing near Gibraltar, others move toward Capri and the Italian Peninsula, while the third great movement of birds of Eastern Europe and Asia is toward Greece and Turkey. If the birds meet storms and contrary winds, many drop exhausted on any island below them. Since spring shooting is permitted, more often than not instead of rest they find death. On Crete, for instance, the coast bristles with guns when the birds are coming north from Africa. Once we snatched, before it could be shot, a little bittern too weary to evade us and released it in a marsh several miles from the gunners. Perhaps that one small bird survived to nest again, but thousands of migrants each spring in that area fall victim to man's protein hunger or to the sportsmen who kill just for fun.

Though countless birds never reach their destination because of exhaustion, storms, or other causes, many are extremely strong fliers. A golden plover can make a nonstop flight between Nova Scotia and South America with a loss of only two ounces of weight.

Large birds that feed chiefly on small mammals and birds, as well as species that sweep the air for insects as they fly, migrate by day. Small birds that forage for insects in trees, bushes, or on the ground drop into convenient thickets at dawn, spend the day feeding and sleeping, then continue their flight as night falls. Seed-eating birds that feed on the ground, especially lark buntings and some sparrows, often assemble in large flocks that move forward over the prairie with a rolling motion as the birds in the rear constantly leapfrog to the forefront of their companions. These birds eat and travel by day, then rest at night. Since most of them make fairly short journeys of a few hundred miles, they do not need to hurry as must the species that travel from South America or distant islands of the ocean.

Some birds that travel very short distances between their wintering places and nesting grounds scarcely appear to migrate at all. Yet those that travel from a valley to a mountain peak may pass through several climatic zones. Birds that travel seasonally up and down mountains are said to make altitudinal migrations. The white-tailed ptarmigan makes such migrations. Those that nest on Logan Pass in Glacier National Park, Montana, eat chiefly willow buds that stand above the snow in wintry valleys; then, as melting snow uncovers suitable food, they move up the mountain slopes to the high alpine meadows where they nest. Many gray-crowned rosy finches that nest in the Tetons may spend the winter in Jackson Hole and, as spring advances up the mountains, follow it to their lofty nesting places in rock crevices near the summit of the towering peaks.

In the Arctic, a few individuals of migratory species will remain through the winter, and a few ravens, willow ptarmigans, and snowy owls may survive the bitter cold. In the northern United States as well, birds sometimes stay during the winter, many of them visiting feeding shelves for sustenance. One winter a Baltimore oriole was seen daily in Hingham, Massachusetts, and a western tanager was once observed in Boston in late December, though they normally winter far to the south. These are only two of many similar strange records.

The birds that remain in the Arctic during the winter, even though the species as a whole is at least slightly migratory, are equipped to survive the rigors of life there. But this is not true of such land birds as orioles, tanagers, and warblers that, because of injury, illness, or lack of instinctive migratory guidance, fail to migrate. Little is known of the history of such aberrant individuals, but it is likely that few survive to make their way once more to their nesting places.

The migratory flight of a bird demands not only an enormous expenditure of energy but special physical capability as well. For example, the breathing apparatus of birds is much more efficient than our own. We breathe about twenty times a minute at rest, and when we exercise, the volume of air inhaled rather than the rate of breathing increases. A pigeon draws about

White Ibis (*Eudocimus albus*)

thirty breaths a minute at rest, but this increases to four hundred and fifty times a minute in flight. In other birds studied, the rate of breathing in flight is correlated, as in pigeons, to the number of wing strokes a minute. At rest a hummingbird breathes two hundred and fifty times a minute. The number of breaths it may take per minute in flight boggles the imagination.

Most birds migrate at rather low altitudes over land areas. At sea level, few fly above three thousand feet, and at night most fly at less than half that altitude. For this reason tall buildings and television towers in the path of migrants pose a grim hazard, particularly on nights when clouds hang low or fog conceals the obstacles in the line of flight. On such a night during spring migration as many as three thousand birds of several species have crashed against the Vertical Assembly Building at the Kennedy Space Center at Cape Canaveral.

Generally, birds migrate rather slowly. Herons fly steadily at less than twenty miles an hour and small land birds travel between twenty and thirty miles per hour, while ducks and geese sustain speeds of forty to fifty miles per hour. Wind and other factors will, of course, affect speed. Often birds idle along, flying in short hops and suddenly, with an abrupt burst of energy, cover as much as one hundred fifty miles in a sustained eight-hour flight. When bar-tailed godwits leave their nesting grounds in Alaska for a winter in New Zealand, they may take as long as two and one-half months for the journey. But when spring approaches they traverse the same distance in half the time of their autumn flight.

It is a pretty fiction that cliff swallows return to the Mission of San Juan Capistrano in California on the same day each year. Nevertheless, it is true that many species arrive at their nesting places with great regularity, the time varying by only a few days year after year. Now and then storms and unseasonable changes in weather have a disastrous effect. One year after a severe March snowstorm in Minnesota, Dr. Thomas Roberts reported that 750,000 Lapland longspurs were counted dead on the ice of two lakes. On the other hand, milder weather fronts often result in spectacular waves of migrants that delight the hearts of bird-watchers. When adverse weather continues for several days, the migrating birds may be halted as if held back by a great dam. Then a sudden rise in temperature and a light, favorable wind break the dam and the multitude of birds plunges forward in a massive wave. If a gentle local rain falls just before dawn, the wave of birds drops down to feed and rest. I remember one spectacular wave flooding the Elmsford Ridge north of New York City. The trees were covered with colorful warblers of a dozen species; orioles darted like orange flames from oak to oak, rose-breasted grosbeaks and wood thrushes shook the air with their melodies, and

in one dogwood at the peak of its bloom five male scarlet tanagers rested. Although the migratory journey is filled with danger and is often wasteful of life, the fit and the fortunate survive to carry on the species.

Even as the internal clock of birds sends them over long and hazardous reaches of land and sea before they come at last to their special nesting places, it also triggers wonderful changes in the outward appearance of many species. Some change from drab winter plumage to bright and sometimes startling colors. Males of many species make use of usually inconspicuous body parts that can only be called ornaments. A male frigatebird expands his red gular pouch to great size, yellow wattles above the eyes of a blue grouse are distended, and a prairie chicken inflates air sacs on the sides of his neck. No matter how odd these may look to us, each fulfills an essential purpose, that of insuring successful reproduction. Without these specialized features, male and female cannot properly communicate and react to each other. They are signals that reach perfection as breeding readiness approaches its climax, an external part of the change taking place within the bodies of birds, and achieve their greatest brilliance and beauty in time for the courtship period. Many species that show little outward sign of change, for their patterns and colors remain the same throughout their adult lives, may go through a molt that gives them their freshest plumage as nesting time approaches.

The most elaborate breeding plumage that most people ever see is the vividly colored train of the male peafowl. In truth there are few birds in the world to rival this exotic bird. Unlike pheasants, turkeys, lyrebirds, and other species that display gorgeous tails, the peafowl's real tail is rather plain, short, and undecorated. His upper tail-coverts form the long train that

Common Puffins (*Fratercula arctica*)

spreads in a magnificent, colorful fan touching the ground on either side of the performer during his display. While watching the peafowl, most people are too bemused to relate the elegance of that bird to the simple breeding-time finery of birds in their own gardens, but even our most common birds bear watching. The house sparrow, actually a weaver finch, has an undistinguished plumage, but as spring approaches a handsome velvet-black bib replaces the wintertime dusky smudge on the throat of the male. Like the train of the peafowl, this fine black bib indicates breeding readiness.

During the winter tanagers, bobolinks, and many warblers have rather obscure plumage but, as the breeding cycle begins, the males assume bright and beautiful feathers. Indigo bunting males are brown in early winter and look much like the females, but as early as January some of them begin to show small

Osprey (*Pandion haliaetus*)

patches of blue which increase in size until by late March most of them are completely blue. Male scarlet tanagers that may winter in far-off Brazil change from dull green plumage, resembling that of the female, to bright scarlet with shining black wings and tail. In early winter bobolinks gathered on the pampas of Argentina look quite alike, but as spring approaches the brown tips on the feathers of the male break off. By the time the bobolink arrives in Florida in early May the male is already decked in spectacular black with white patches on the back and a large buffy-yellow one on the nape and back of the head.

Though many birds make a startling transformation in their plumage for the breeding season, others undergo less dramatic changes. The spotted sandpiper merely adds large, dark spots to its breast, and the black-bellied plover acquires a black front, living up to its name during the breeding time only. The red on the belly of male red-bellied woodpeckers is often so pale in winter that it is overlooked by casual observers, but it becomes conspicuous at nesting time. Many small gulls, including the Franklin's gull, the abundant black-headed gull of Europe, and the beautiful swallow-tailed gull of the Galápagos Islands, have pale heads in winter, then wear dark hoods in the breeding season. Many species of terns have whitish heads in winter; then, as the courtship season advances, they develop black caps as shining as satin.

Some birds signal readiness to breed by changes in the color of their unfeathered skin or by newly intense colors and sizes of wattles, lappets, caruncles, and fleshy "horns." These changes may be as slight as the thin red line around the eyes and at the jaw of a California gull or as extensive as the pouch of a male frigatebird. Domestic turkeys, like their wild turkey relatives, have wrinkled, bare heads that change from grayish-blue to red as they perform before females, and finally fade until almost white as they become exhausted by their vigorous dancing. The colors of bare skin as well as the bill and legs of a bird can tell us much about their internal state, as you can see in the plate on page 96. Fred Truslow's camera caught the never-before-photographed blush of a pair of least bitterns meeting after an absence, a sign of stress that receded as quickly as it appeared.

Not all birds signal breeding readiness by acquiring special plumage or flesh colors but keep the same appearance throughout the year. With their first feathers, young blue jays and killdeer, for example, look like their parents, while a trumpeter swan requires about three years to achieve adult plumage and a bald eagle may be four or more years old before it has a white head and tail. Once they have adult plumage, these species and many others keep it for the rest of their lives, though it is renewed at intervals by molting.

Breeding changes among some birds go unnoticed

except by the extremely observant. Of all the birds in the world, only skimmers have a lower mandible that is much longer than the upper one. The American black skimmer, the largest of the three skimmers in the world, has the most colorful bill; the half nearest the face is red, the tip half is black. Acute observers will note that the red part of the bill brightens as the breeding season approaches. A slight change can be noted in wood storks, whose feet are always pink but briefly, during the ardor of courtship, flush to a deeper peach-blossom color. Puffins undergo a much more radical change in preparation for courtship. At the end of the nesting season they go to sea with an ashy breast, a dull black back, and a dark lumpy bill, but during midwinter they renew their plumage. The back becomes shiny black, as do the crown and a wide band drawn forward across the front of the neck, while the breast and belly gleam like snow. Most startling is the big rainbow sheath that develops over the bill. A fine red line separates the feathers from this huge sheath, the inner half of which is bluish-gray and outlined in ivory or yellow. The outer half is largely fire-engine red, but the color is not even; ridged lines that follow the curve of the sheath are red mixed with yellow. The *pièce de résistance* of this enormous sheath is the large, fleshy roseate of vivid orange decorating the jaws.

Sometimes the change of plumage has aroused the cupidity of man. In no family of birds did it cause more havoc than among the herons and egrets; some barely escaped extinction at the hands of hunters who sought their plumes. The great egret's covering is always snowy white, from the natal down through the juvenile stage to nuptial plumage, but as the breeding season arrives, its elegant white feathers are enhanced by snowy plumes that spring forth and then are shed like the petals of a flower when their purpose has been fulfilled. Forty or more long plumes spread across the middle of the back and, when fully developed, extend several inches beyond the end of the tail. At the same time, short, delicate plumes make a frill below the base of the neck; these are lifted and fanned at moments of intense emotion, forming a misty cloud. The black legs of the great egret show little or no change at breeding time, but the face changes radically. The long bill deepens from yellow to ochre, and on the upper mandible is a light brushing of black. The yellow lores (the space between the eyes and the edge of the upper mandible) and a narrow band of bare skin around the eyes change to bright lime green, which deepens in

White Pelicans (*Pelecanus erythrorynchos*)

tone as nesting progresses. The lemon-yellow iris is ringed with a hair-thin line of black.

For months, birds associate in large groups without animosity toward each other, or they live solitary lives, preoccupied with the search for food and escape from enemies. Suddenly their lives change. Vast numbers of birds, billions of them, leap into the sky and move away from their winter homes on southern continents and islands and on the oceans. They stream toward the temperate and arctic zones of the north. All of them move according to a mysterious guidance that we do not understand but regard with wonder as the birds unerringly steer toward their distant goals, inexorably tied to the dictates of time, which compels them to make their annual journeys. All are obedient to the laws of their kind. They have no control over the changes in their bodies, changes that occur as regularly as the passage of the seasons. They can only submit to the demands created by those changes in their bodies.

> . . . every year hath its winter,
>   And every year hath its rain—
> But a day is always coming
>   When the birds go north again.
>
> —Ella Higginson, 1862-1940

Claim a Territory, Win a Mate

If a garden is planted with trees and shrubs that provide food and shelter and is supplied with water for drinking and bathing, it will soon be "owned" by several species of birds. The boundaries each species zealously protects do not coincide exactly with each other, or, for that matter, with the limits of your garden. But to each species its boundaries are distinct and are defended fiercely at breeding time. In my one-acre garden in the southern United States, a nesting pair each of mockingbirds, cardinals, red-bellied woodpeckers, mourning doves, screech owls, Carolina wrens, great-crested flycatchers, and chuck-will's-widows maintain ownership each spring. The first six species are present throughout the year, while the last two arrive from as far away as South America when the nesting season approaches.

These birds coexist peacefully because their requirements for nesting places and food do not conflict. Insect grazers of the shrubs and trees pay no attention to the seed and fruit eaters. Both the great-crested flycatcher and the chuck-will's-widow eat flying insects, but catch them differently. The flycatcher perches on an open twig from which it darts into the air to catch a passing insect with an audible snap of its bill, while the chuck-will's-widow cruises to and fro at dawn and dusk with its great mouth wide open, scooping up insects as it flies. The screech owls hunt at night for large insects and small mammals while the other birds are resting.

Many birds have more than one kind of territory during the course of the year, but here we are concerned only with the territory occupied during the nesting cycle. This well-defined and defended area has several functions: it provides a place to woo a mate and to establish a reasonably secure nesting site that has sufficient shelter, nesting material, and food to protect and support the future family. Should another individual of the same species attempt an invasion, there would be an immediate battle, for nowhere in the animal world are territorial fights more frequent, more determined, and more lasting than they are among birds during the nesting season.

Territorial claims, quarrels, and insistence on domination are most intense at the beginning of the season when the birds first arrive on their nesting areas, for this is the time when each bird must prove his claim. The males usually arrive on suitable nesting habitats first, with the experienced older birds in the vanguard so they are able to establish their claims to the finest sites, perhaps the very ones they owned the previous year. Males are followed by the females, who, more often than not, choose the territory they like best and then accept the male who has won it. Unless the population of a given species has fallen to a dangerous low, its numbers through the normal annual increases are greater than the available rich sites; there are never enough of the best quality. Thus there are always unmated, wandering individuals to fill in if an accident occurs to one or both birds in a good territory. Among red-winged blackbirds, the male with the richest territory in a marsh may win several mates to share his abundance, while a young or ineffectual red-wing, who must settle for a poor location at the edge of the marsh, may win only a single female or none at all.

Birds rarely stray outside the normal range of their own species when choosing a nesting territory. We expect to find a parula warbler nesting in a northern conifer forest draped with usnea lichen. A prothonotary warbler is expected to claim a territory in a moist woodland south of Chesapeake Bay in the eastern part of the United States (though for many years it has been a rare but regular nesting species in northern New York), where it will be the only warbler to nest in an old woodpecker hole or the cavity of a decaying stump. A puffin will select a site only on an island in northern seas, while a limpkin nests in a southern freshwater marsh. It is useless to imagine any species of North American woodpecker claiming a nesting territory that lacks trees in which it can chisel a hole, or a gannet nesting far from the ocean. The kind of habitat where each species claims and defends a territory is determined instinctively, an inheritance handed down by a long line of ancestors.

Territories vary in size according to the species. In order to breed successfully, a pair of golden eagles in the western United States requires many square miles. In a spruce forest infested by a bad outbreak of budworm, a bay-breasted warbler may need no more than a half acre for its family, though the majority of songbirds probably need an acre or more, depending on its quality.

The shape of a territory depends on the contour of the area, though observers have noted that oval outlines are often preferred. Circumstances often force variations of this shape. Kingfishers may dig their burrows in sheer banks left when sand has been excavated some distance from water and then claim as much as half a mile of shore, completely ignoring the land between the nest and the shore.

Colonial birds have the smallest territories since they gather nesting materials and food in other locations, often some distance away. There are no fish in Great Salt Lake, Utah, so white pelicans nesting on its islands travel as far as eighty miles or more on fishing expeditions to distant bodies of water. They are not quarrelsome birds and build their nests so close together that they could easily jab each other without standing up. Cliff swallows, too, enjoy the company of their own kind and I have never seen conflict among them, although their mud nests are jammed tightly together beneath the eaves of buildings and on cliffs. They also travel away from their nests to feed—over lakes when damselflies are emerging or over fields when flying ants take to the air in clouds.

On a dike of the Bear River Migratory Bird Refuge in Utah a group of California gulls nest in a congested colony each summer. When the gulls first arrive, the dike is a scene of chaotic confusion as they swirl about, screaming incessantly. Each gull is in a state of frantic excitement that increases as more and more gulls arrive, but within a few days the confusion disappears and the apparently aimless activity has been sorted into a well-organized community with an orderly spacing between pairs. Order is maintained so long as one gull remains on guard at each nest; the moment a nest is left undefended another gull may swoop in to take possession, steal nesting material, or even eat eggs or young.

In a gannet colony, territories are even smaller than those in a gull colony. A gannet returning from a fish-

ing expedition usually makes a precise landing within its tiny territory, but occasionally one fails to do so, through misjudgment or confusion. As it makes its way through the crowded colony, it becomes a veritable whipping boy, a victim of blows from each gannet through whose territory it must pass to reach its own nest.

So strong is the respect for territorial rights among birds that a neighbor trying to expand its claim is usually driven back easily. Occasionally the furious defender fails to note that he has pursued the guilty intruder beyond his own boundary, and instantly the intruder becomes the protector of his own property. So the struggle seesaws until each bird returns to its respective territory. Whether the area is as large as that of a golden eagle or as small as that of a gannet, once the boundaries are established and accepted by neighboring birds, something like peaceful coexistence is established.

Birds have a limited series of sounds that they use in communicating with their own kind, although recent studies of taped bird sounds prove that almost all birds have a far greater vocabulary than was believed when we depended on our ears alone. They may communicate vocally or by making instrumental sounds by tapping as woodpeckers do or beating the wings very rapidly as ruffed grouse do, or as a nighthawk makes a booming sound as it plunges downward, then brakes abruptly and zooms upward, forcing the wind through

Yellow-headed Blackbird (*Xanthocephalus xanthocephalus*)

21

its primaries. Birds also have a highly developed system of alternatives to sound, such as postures and attitudes, signals recognized by their own species and indispensable to a successful life. Like the primitive gestures we use to communicate with other people whose language we do not know, certain signals can be understood by all birds. The excited calls of a blue jay when it finds a snake, owl, or cat in its territory will attract birds of many species and cause them to assemble and even mob the enemy. Widely separated vultures circling high in the sky recognize the signal when food has been discovered by one of them, and they converge to share the feast. These signals are recognized by people as well as by the birds that hear the blue jays or see the vultures. Some signals are used throughout the year, but others employed during the breeding season only are usually more varied and complex.

Songbirds usually have several singing perches spaced around the periphery of their claims and from these prominent posts shout their ownership of the territory. Adjacent birds join in, each doing his best to sing more emphatically than the others, each indicating where he lives and announcing in his own way to other males of this species, "This is my territory! Stay out!" At the same time he is announcing to females that he will be the best mate and that his is the best territory, a splendid place to rear a family. Nonsinging birds make their territorial ownership known in various other ways. Woodpeckers drum, a western grebe puts his head close to the water and swims quickly at any intruder, a Canada goose hisses and strikes, and a mourning dove lifts and snaps one wing as a threat. Sustained as territorial warfare is, more often than not it is carried on without bloodshed or even bodily contact.

Like the defense of territory, the courtship of birds is active, intense, and sometimes violent. Among the approximately eight thousand species of birds in the world, there is an incredible variety of courting behavior. Each species has its own ritualized form of courting and by repeating the ritual often, particularly when one of the pair returns after an absence, the bond is strengthened. Sometimes this ritual involves feeding, and sometimes the presentation of sticks, which may or may not be used as nesting material. There are mutual displays ranging from simple or complex in which both sexes take part; sometimes only the male displays before the female, while in other species the female displays for the male. Among some species, including prairie chickens and ruffs, males congregate on a communal display ground and females come to watch their performance and to choose a mate from among the actors. The most admired male may mate with several

Snowy Egret (*Egretta thula*)

22

females. Often a female is attracted to an especially good territory, and when she enters it the male may accept her or he may drive her away.

We have already mentioned the fine patterns, colors, and spectacular ornaments that some birds display at nesting time, but these are only part of the courtship proceedings. Many birds have special calls, songs, and mechanical sounds; some have special display arenas, and many perform exhibition flights and rituals for which we have no name except dancing. In fact, there is an almost infinite variety of signals used by birds in establishing and protecting their territories and winning their mates; for each sex of each species recognizes its own kind and only by means of these stylized rituals and signals can mating be accomplished. To prove the unique role that signals play, a group of ornithologists disrupted the family life of a pair of yellow-shafted flickers. The male of this species has a black mustache mark while the female does not. The experimenters trapped the female, attached a black paper mustache to her head, and restored her to the nest. Her returning mate swept toward her but when he saw the false mustache, instant consternation erupted. Furiously he attacked her and drove her from the territory.

Many scientists who observe birds in their natural surroundings suspect that an affection similar to that between people may link couples in a pair bond. By no means are all pair bonds formed on or even near the nesting site. Some birds form strong attachments long before they are old enough to breed. Bearded tits become engaged when only two and one-half months old, nearly a year before they make their first nest, and many youthful geese form similar attachments. Old-squaws carry on excited courtships on Long Island Sound and other open waters before they leave for their arctic nesting grounds. Though these and many other ducks form pair bonds months before nesting time, the pairs separate soon after arriving at the nest site. It is believed that some birds, swans and geese, for instance, mate for life. European white storks are monogamous and annually return to the same nest with the same mate as long as they live. But barn swallows that have more than one brood each season may change mates between each brood. House wrens are polygamous, and one of these little birds may have a harem of half a dozen females, each one busy with the care of eggs or young. Hummingbirds do not form pairs at all, but after ritualized display copulate and separate immediately.

Most birds, even pelicans and loons, have moments of grace and beauty in courtship, but are also given to unusual antics at this time. They skylark, strut, bow, bill and quiver the wings, display their fancy feathers, plumes, and colors, or balloon their pouches or sacs. To our eyes, these capers often look ludicrous, yet each is necessary for communication. But no matter how ardent and persuasive a male may be, the female he courts must have reached the right stage in her own cycle before she is physically able to respond.

When both sexes look alike, another difficulty arises. A female who sees an area to her liking will drop out of a migrating flock and, hearing the exultant song of a male, enter his territory. Concentrating on the defense of his newly established territory, the male sees the intruder, who resembles himself, and rushes at his look-alike belligerently. If the female is ready for a mate she may move away at first, but she will return persistently until she finally pacifies his wrath. Then she is likely to join her mate in securing his borders and driving away other females as well as males who seek to intrude on the territory.

The males of many songbird species are very beautiful, with striking patterns and spectacular colors, but appearance alone is not always enough to win a female. Among colorful wood warblers, both American and painted redstarts add to their beauty by fanning their bright wings and tails during courtship. A red-winged blackbird bows low and flares his yellow-edged red epaulettes, while a yellow-headed blackbird contorts himself into a strange shape as he expels an agonized wail.

Usually when the female of any species is more brightly colored than the male, she is the one who does the courting, sometimes winning the attention of more than one male. The phalaropes are well known for this

Reddish Egret (*Dichromanassa rufescens*)

23

reversal of the usual behavior and appearance among birds; the female's responsibilities are limited to courtship and to laying the eggs in the nest prepared for them by the male, who then incubates the eggs and later cares for the young birds.

Plainly garbed mockingbirds look alike, but they make the best of their gray and white plumage when courting by facing each other in a dance: they sashay to the right and then to the left in unison, flicking their wings so the white patches flash and vanish rapidly. Spoonbills, too, look alike, and when the female is ready to mate, she selects a perch where she may later build a nest. She shakes twigs and leaves with her bill whenever another spoonbill appears. When a male is attracted to the conspicuously perched female, he flies to her and tries to perch beside her, gently jerking his head up and down. He threatens any other spoonbill that comes near and often lunges at it. Even though the female clearly indicates her readiness to accept a mate, she usually rejects his first advances. Though they look alike, they recognize each other by sight as soon as she accepts the male. How do they know each other? And why do unmated males that now approach her seem aware that she is already mated? Why are they so easily put to flight by the chosen male? These are unanswered questions that continue to puzzle observers.

Ruffed grouse have no difficulty in recognizing the opposite sex, for the female is a plain mottled brown, while his appearance is quite dramatic as he goes into his display. Mounting his favorite log—a display arena from which he drives other males—he droops his wings and fans his tail until he resembles a miniature turkey. He elevates the ruff around his neck and, shaking his head from side to side, continues the performance by cupping his lifted wings and fanning the air, slowly at first and then faster and faster until they make a roaring sound. Woodcock, too, display in solitary arenas to which they attract females. The male's loud *peent* can be heard for some distance and while the sky is still luminous with the afterglow of sunset, the woodcock mounts into the air, sweeping up and up in widening spirals accompanied by a winnowing sound. This music is made as the air whips through his wing feathers. Soon a sweet twittering drifts down from the circling bird, and then the woodcock himself drifts down as erratically as a falling leaf. There is control, however, for he nearly always lands close to the place from which he launched his extraordinary flight. If not disturbed by an observer, the woodcock repeats this ritual over and over again until the last light has faded from the sky.

Many birds, especially those that live in open places with few trees or bushes, make daytime flights above their territories. Sprague's pipits soar above the western prairies until they become mere specks among the clouds and circle there, sending their faint trills and quavering melodies to earth. I timed one Sprague's pipit flight that lasted for forty-two minutes. Horned larks sing their twittering songs as they fly above the meadows and golf courses where they nest. Wordsworth delighted in the skylarks that mount into the air to welcome the dawn, yet the aerial songs of many of our birds are equally worthy of appreciation by poets.

Both gulls and gannets, whose voices are more often raucous than melodious, do a great deal of billing during courtship. That is, they strike their bills together and nibble each other's neck and head. Pelicans, herons, and spoonbills often present sticks as gifts. Terns present small silvery fish that have the advantage of being edible, as are the seeds that a male cardinal often gives its mate. A Franklin's gull will cough up and deposit in the mouth of his prospective bride a very special gift—a ball of partly digested food.

All herons make a big show in courtship of fluffing their feathers so their bodies look greatly enlarged. The neck appears swollen and is stretched upward while the bill is snapped. When performed by a reddish egret, this display is very comic, for as the reddish feathers and rusty plumes bristle and are shaken forward around the face, the bird looks for all the world as if a bedraggled mop had been put on its head.

Some woodpecker pairs, especially flickers, hitch themselves jerkily up the trunk of a tree in unison, swaying their heads from side to side. They nod and bow, sometimes circling the trunk of the tree as they climb upward. Their lively activity is usually accompanied by loud cries of *wick, wick,* which to John Burroughs was one of the loveliest sounds of spring. Flickers have a wide variety of calls, but their most emphatic spring love song, an instrumental sound, is made by drumming on drainpipes, metal caps on poles, hollow limbs, or whatever object provides the greatest resonance. Flickers return to favorite drumming places for the duration of the courting season, usually at dawn, and strike blows so rapidly they sound like a continuous roll.

Pursuit flights are indulged in by many species of birds. Coy females, especially among passerine birds, may entice the male to chase them, and ducks, too, are often pursued by one or more drakes. White-throated swifts come together briefly and revolve like pinwheels for a few breathtaking seconds. This action by the small swift is exciting but cannot equal the drama of courtship by bald eagles. These majestic raptors still nest in Florida, but their numbers are sadly diminished now. In former days when mate greeted mate upon their return to nest in late autumn, it was not unusual to hear their high, shrill cries. The great birds traced vast circles beneath the clouds, then rushed together, reaching out their powerful claws; and with clasped talons they tumbled in a dizzy whirl, only to break apart and resume their circling flight and shrill cries.

Nest Building

The nest of a bird is in no way the equivalent of a human home. We build a house to live in; birds do not. Their nests are built specifically to hold eggs and, in many species, to rear the young, an activity often shared by both sexes. The embryos of birds, having only a shell for protection, require special provision as those of mammals do not, since their embryos are protected in the womb of the female.

Many birds are skillful in camouflaging their nests by building them of materials that blend inconspicuously into the surroundings and placing them where they are not likely to attract the attention of predators. We are aware of how successful they are when we walk through a forest that is alive with singing birds yet seldom see a nest unless we make a diligent search. Rather than construct hidden nests, some species provide safety from danger by building on top of very tall trees, on inaccessible cliffs, on islands, or under ground. Others crowd together in great colonies as if they were aware that in numbers lies protection for the individual.

Fossils of birds indicate that they have been on earth for at least 160 million years. Over that vast passage of time, great changes have taken place in the earth—in its appearance, in its climate, and in the life on it. Occasionally there have been sudden cataclysmic happenings, but most changes have been almost imperceptible, so slow they were of trivial importance from year to year. Geological records show how great, with the passage of millennia, were the modifications wrought by changing temperatures, by wind, rain, and shifting of rocks. Yet these changes were so slow that many plants and animals were able to adapt to them; those that did not faded away into extinction.

The slowly changing world gave most forms of life time enough to adjust to new conditions. Adaptations made by birds astonish us with the variety of bills, legs, toes, wings, and feathers that help them meet the varied conditions of their lives. From the tiny bee hummingbird that weighs less than two grams to the three-hundred-pound ostrich, from the brown kiwi with only flightless, vestigial wings to the wandering albatross with a wingspan up to eleven feet and more, the bodies of birds have modified to meet changing situations and ways of life.

With few exceptions, birds manage without tools other than those provided by some body part. An Egyptian vulture occasionally uses a stone to break the thick shell of an ostrich egg, and a woodpecker finch on the Galápagos Islands may pluck a cactus spine and use it to probe in a hole too deep for it to reach a grub or a spider with its bill. But almost all birds have only their own bodies with which to accomplish many extraordinary tasks.

Each species of bird is unique in its nesting habits, and experts can often identify the owner of a nest by noting only the habitat, the nest's location, shape, and size, and the materials used to build it. When a nest is in a shrub or tree one must note whether it is placed in a crotch, on a limb or slung beneath it, near the trunk or close to the end of a branch among the leaves. Some nests are marvelously complicated. The bee hummingbird skillfully constructs an exquisite nest of plant down and spider silk. The long-tailed tailorbird sews leaves into a cup, which she then lines with soft fibers and plant down to make a cradle for her eggs. For thread she uses plant fibers or spider silk, and each evenly spaced stitch is carefully tied before the next one is pulled through. No less impressive is the monumental nest built by the bald eagle. One thirty-five-year-old nest in Ohio was estimated to contain almost two tons of material when at last it crashed to the ground. The finest gliding bird in the world, the wandering albatross, is believed to nest only every other year; then it builds a high pile of plant material in the shape of a volcano and makes a depression in the top of it for its single egg.

Some birds build no nest at all. Most cowbirds, and this is true of both species that live in the United States, search for nests of other species that lay eggs about the size of theirs, and when the nest attendant is absent, the female cowbird sneaks in and lays an egg, leaving it to be cared for by foster parents. As many as three brown-headed cowbird eggs have been found in a single Brewer's sparrow nest. Many people believe their parasitizing of Kirtland's warbler nests is the foremost reason for the declining numbers of this endangered species. Yellow warblers are frequently parasitized by cowbirds and sometimes bury an unwanted egg under a layer of nesting material, creating a second-story nest over it. Dr. Edward Howe Forbush wrote of a six-story nest with a cowbird egg in every one of them. European cuckoos are also parasitic, but American cuckoos build their own nests and care for their own young.

Nighthawks, whip-poor-wills, and chuck-will's-widows of the United States and nightjars of Central and South America simply lay their two white eggs on the ground. These species are closely related, but they are not alone in their lack of a nest-building instinct. The male ostrich, the world's largest bird, which may stand six feet tall, does most of the incubation of the eggs laid by the members of his harem. Several females may lay in a single clutch, and it is said they sometimes make a shallow scrape for the eggs, though I have seen no evidence of this in East Africa, where the eggs are simply pushed together for incubation. Murres, called guillemots in Europe, lay their eggs on bare ledges just above the reach of the pounding waves, yet each knows its own tiny territory and its own egg though the rock shelf is tightly crowded with other murres.

Puffins that breed off the Maine coast on Machias Seal Island lay their single egg under great boulders above the reach of storm tides, usually placing them on bare stones but occasionally adding four or five straws as if an impulse to build a nest still lingered in their behavior. On islands off Newfoundland, northern Europe, and around the British Isles, puffins often dig burrows as long as a man's arm in the soft turf, and may carry into these a billful of grass to make a primitive nest. When a widely detached population of a species adopts a different way of life from the majority of its kind, we catch a glimmer of the way birds have changed through the ages.

Like some puffins and all burrowing owls, the little kiwi of New Zealand digs a burrow in the ground for its single egg. The kiwi is a strange bird that cannot fly at all; its vestigial wings are only about two and a half inches long and its nostrils are on the tip of its bill. It lays the largest egg in proportion to its size of any bird in the world.

When a female common tern sits on the sand and turns to face her mate as he circles around her, teasingly holding a small fish in his bill, she makes a shallow scrape or scoop that becomes her nest. Sometimes she adds a few bits of broken seashells, but many of these terns make no attempt to embellish the simple receptacle for the eggs. In the Central Pacific, a fairy tern places its single egg in the crotch of a tree. Black terns usually nest in marshes, but on some potholes in Montana their nests are virtually floating islands anchored to tall weeds growing far out in the water. Arctic terns make scrapes if they nest on sand, but on Matinicus Rock off the Maine coast they choose a crevice in a rock, usually one where some vegetation has gained a foothold. After matting down this vegetation, they add more plant material and press it into a shallow cup. On this particular island the terns live in a noisy, compact colony, while in Alaska they are often solitary nesting birds, one pair to a marsh or lake shore. On the Dry Tortugas, noddy terns build firm platforms of seaweed and sticks in the mangroves. Roseate terns, which have an almost cosmopolitan distribution, look very much like common terns and sometimes nest with them, but while the common terns nest in the open sand, the roseate terns usually hide their nests under beach grass or other vegetation.

Oystercatchers, and many other shorebirds that breed on beaches and dunes, often make scrape nests. Loons have advanced somewhat beyond the simplest of scrape nests. A female loon squirms about in excitement when the male approaches and often throws around bits of moss, lichen, and other plant material.

Black-legged Kittiwakes (*Rissa tridactyla*)

Later she pulls some of this into the depression made by her movements so a definite nest is formed.

Many ground-nesting birds build well-constructed, beautifully lined nests. Horned larks, lark buntings, and longspurs nest on the vast grass prairies, while water pipits prefer high alpine meadows, but all line their nests with soft, fine plant materials. Ruffed grouse choose the forest floor, where the female blends inconspicuously into the dead leaves. Many sparrows nest on the ground; fox sparrows usually near wet places, vesper sparrows in dry fields, white-throated sparrows in conifer forests, while the endangered dusky seaside sparrow nests only in a very restricted area of salt-marsh grass and salicornia in central Brevard County, Florida. In the Everglades National Park in Florida, Fred Truslow once found, nesting on the ground, a barred owl that normally nests in cavities of deciduous trees. In the same area he also photographed a great horned owl nesting on the ground among fallen pine needles. When trees are absent, great horned owls often nest on the ledges of great cliffs for security. This nest built on the ground under pine trees suitable for nesting was truly unique.

The scrape nests undoubtedly originated from the movements made by the females as they turned about on the ground during courtship, and it is easy to understand their development from such simple beginnings to the careful lining of the scrapes for extra comfort in incubation as well as added protection for the eggs. But the origin of complicated nests remains a mystery. How did Baltimore orioles learn to weave their intricate hanging nests? What caused pied-billed grebes to make floating nests? Why did burrowing owls decide to nest underground? We can only wonder at the infinite variety of birds' nests and at the skills of birds that, having only a bill, feet, and wings to work with, are yet able to construct, often very quickly, complicated nests in which to lay their eggs.

Most nests are built of plant materials readily available in a bird's own territory—fine plant down and fibers, grasses, sticks of varied sizes, or seaweed, which carried to the nest soaking wet and limp, becomes stiff when it is dry. Animal materials are also used—insect and spider silk, fur, wool, feathers, and shed snakeskins. Little cave swiftlets in the Orient make their entire nests out of gluelike secretions from their own salivary glands. Incidentally, these nests form the basis for the consommé-like soup that many people enjoy.

Many birds are attracted to exceptional materials. An oriole may interlace its nest with strands of bright, many-colored yarns. Crows snatch bright objects so often it is not surprising to find a thimble or a gold ring in one of their nests. I have heard of a robin's nest with a dollar bill woven into it, and eagles have been known to add such oddities as children's toys, light bulbs, shoes, Clorox bottles, magazines, and even silk un-

Osprey (*Pandion haliaetus*)

derpants to their massive nests. In a recent collection of his letters, E. B. White wrote of a warbler's nest made of fox fur, which he had found near his home in Maine. On the National Bison Range in Montana I once found an eastern kingbird nest made, appropriately enough, of bison fur. Male phainopeplas do most of the nest building for their species, and almost always include some flower petals as decoration, but these are probably a traditional part of nest building for this species rather than an accidental addition of available materials as the others appear to be.

Many species of birds use mud in their nests. Robins make a rough framework of rather coarse sticks and form a mud cup inside this, which they line with fine, soft fibers and rootlets. The closely packed colonial nests of cliff swallows are made of mud mixed with saliva. One of the pleasant sights of spring is a group of these swallows gathering mud from puddles in dirt roads, by streams, or on flooded fields. With wings fluttering, they poke their short bills into the mud, fill them up, and then pile more on top. Each makes hundreds of trips before enough mud has been collected to build its jug-shaped nest. Cliff swallows once built their nests exclusively on sheer cliffs, but now most of them have moved to man-made structures, placing the nests close to the roof where the overhang provides protection from the weather.

In Argentina, rufous horneros (often called ovenbirds) are, like cliff swallows, about six inches long, but they make nests of mud that may weigh as much as eight pounds each. These nests, shaped like the outdoor ovens still used by some families in French Canada and in Argentina, are usually saddled on sturdy limbs, but I have seen them perched like caps on fence posts. Once dry, these nests are as hard and durable as cement.

Many shorebirds, of course, nest close to water, some on sea beaches or near estuaries, others on inland marshes, by lakes and streams, or in artificial impoundments. A snowy plover is equally at home on a Texas beach or on the blazing sand of dry areas of the Bear River delta at Great Salt Lake. Avocets usually choose a dry area sparsely covered with tawny grass, while black-necked stilts nest nearby but where the ground is soggy and plant growth is rich. Stilts sometimes lose their eggs when water rises and floods the nests. Many birds, such as rails, bitterns, and gallinules, nest in marshes or at the edges of ponds and streams. If the water rises a few inches, their eggs, too, may be lost. Sandhill cranes use better judgment, for they nest on high, firm tussocks, piling them even higher with marsh vegetation.

White pelicans and often brown pelicans, too, as well as many species of cormorants and gulls, nest on the ground on islands, where they are relatively safe from predators. Although there may be ample space to spread out, these birds usually huddle together. But probably no birds in the world nest so close together as sooty, royal, and elegant terns, and gannets; each pair has little more than a square foot of ground for its nest.

Natural cavities in trees are used as nest sites by many species, but especially popular are the cavities chiseled by woodpeckers. These holes extend toward the center of the trunk or large limb, then downward in a sort of pear shape. Some woodpeckers are so attached to a particular tree that they chisel a new nest

American Avocet (*Recurvirostra americana*)

hole in it year after year until at last the tree decays and falls. In this book you will find Fred Truslow's remarkable photographs (pages 80–81) of a pileated woodpecker in the act of carrying away its eggs after the tree in which the nest had been dug broke off. Having reared a family in a particular hole, a woodpecker will then abandon it, but it is quickly occupied by other hole-nesting species that cannot make holes for themselves. When several holes have been made in a single tree, it becomes a bird apartment house. In a small coulee in the National Bison Range in western Montana, a few trees stand in an otherwise treeless area. Five species of woodpecker nest on the Range, but only two of them—flickers and Lewis' woodpeckers—have made cavities in this small half-acre coulee. One spring when these two pairs of woodpeckers were busy feeding their young, mountain bluebirds, black-capped chickadees, starlings, tree swallows, house wrens, and kestrels were busy with eggs or young in holes made in previous years by the woodpeckers.

Many species of birds nest on cliffs, ledges, and even in caves. The shelving rock of the great Hudson River Palisades, facing New York City, once provided safe nesting places for the now rare peregrine falcons, and they still nest on the cliffs along the south coast of England. Narrow ledges of islands rising abruptly from the ocean furnish nesting sites for many sea birds, including gannets, gulls, murres, and dovekies. Ospreys and bald eagles occasionally choose high crags instead of trees for their nests. Inside the entrance to some caves in Texas and New Mexico, cave swallows make their nests in small colonies and share the space with a pair of canyon wrens and even a pair of adaptable great horned owls.

Many birds have taken advantage of man-made structures for their nests. We are accustomed to phoebes that nest under bridges, but it is surprising to find dippers nesting among the girders supporting bridges over rapid streams. A few years ago a pair of peregrine falcons nested on the window ledge of a fashionable hotel in New York. Unfortunately, cities more often harbor less glamorous species such as starlings, house sparrows, and pigeons, all introduced from Europe by people who failed to consider the harm that such introductions could produce. Instead of their native cliffs, the pigeons nest on window ledges. The house sparrows often push their nests into lighted signs, gaining some artificial heat. Starlings roost in such hordes in some of our cities that they are a plague, and when spring comes they stuff their nests in whatever crevices they can find. Chimney swifts have abandoned hollow trees for our chimneys. Barn owls, both in our country and in Britain, often nest in belfry towers of churches. Blue jays, usually secretive about their nests, occasionally become as bold about nesting as they are at a feeding shelf. One pair of jays chose to nest on an apartment-house fire escape close to a busy street and a railroad. In spite of the exposed location, this pair reared their young successfully for three years in a row in that peculiar situation.

Dr. Herbert Stoddard once kept a record of a pair of Carolina wrens on a Georgia plantation that succeeded in raising their young in a tractor in daily use around the fields. Dr. Austin Rand, former Curator of Birds at the Chicago Natural History Museum, observed some tree swallows that tucked their nests into small openings of a ferry boat that traveled across the Saint Lawrence River between Ogdensburg, New York, and Prescott, Canada. Not at all disturbed as the boat pulled into piers in different countries, the swallows gathered nesting materials from either shore and later fed their young on American and Canadian insects. National boundaries meant nothing to them.

City parks, gardens, and farmyards have provided ideal conditions for many species, including cardinals and mockingbirds. Old fields grown up to bushes have provided added nesting places for chestnut-sided warblers, so their numbers are greater than in colonial days. Where miles and miles of grain fields have supplanted the once varied vegetation, an ideal habitat for undesirable multitudes of blackbirds has been created at the expense of man, who finds the blackbirds are a plague that devours his crops. When winter comes the same blackbirds create a nuisance in some urban areas. On the other hand, changes in the habitat have reduced other species such as the whooping crane and the California condor and may have caused the extinction of the ivory-billed woodpecker.

Most birds that nest in shrubs and trees build sturdy structures to withstand storms that shake and twist their supports. Yellow warblers favor crotches in dense shrubbery so the nest is supported on two or more sides. A wood thrush saddles its nest on a sturdy limb, while a golden-crowned kinglet places its nest among the dense needles near the end of a conifer branch. Eastern kingbirds prefer a tall bush or tree in an open area in which they build durable nests with a commanding view so the incubating bird can detect any predator approaching and sally forth to attack it. Northern parula warblers in spruce forests tuck their nests into thick strands of usnea lichen, where they are so thoroughly concealed that I have rarely found one until the parents began to come and go at short intervals to feed their young. When strong winds blow the two-foot-long hanging nest of a Lichtenstein's oriole or the four- to five-foot nest of a crested oropendola, swinging them in wide arcs, it is rare for either to be wrenched from its firm lashing to the limb of a tree. The ten-inch nest of a tiny bushtit is usually protected by the dense branches in which it is hung. This nest is particularly beautiful; formed of various plant fibers, down, and moss, it is securely bound to several twigs.

The eggs are laid in a soft little cup at the bottom of the snug structure.

Many songbirds build cuplike nests, but variations in size, shape, and location are great. A vermilion flycatcher attaches its flat, saucerlike nest, made of plant down, lichens, and spider silk, to a horizontal limb of a tree, where it looks like a small knot, a part of the limb itself. In contrast, a yellow-headed blackbird's nest is almost as deep as a bowl, made of grasses and weeds, lined with finer grasses, and attached securely to swaying rushes or cattails. In the same kind of habitat, a long-billed marsh wren contrives a dome over its otherwise cuplike nest and makes an entrance at the side. The energetic male of this species builds nest after nest, sometimes half a dozen. His mate may reject all of them and make one herself out of grasses and reeds, lining it with feathers and cattail down. A truly amazing nest is constructed by the four-and-one-half-inch verdin, a close relative of the chickadee, which nests in the chaparral and desert areas of the American Southwest. It gathers thorny twigs, forming them into a hollow mass almost the size of a football, which is attached near the end of a prickly branch. This is stuffed with leaves and grasses, then lined with feathers and soft, matted plant fibers. The side entrance, also lined with soft material, flares slightly like the mouth of a small jug. That so tiny a bird can build a nest larger than itself without being impaled by the formidable materials it uses or the spines in its location seems miraculous.

The construction of a bird's nest may take a few days or several weeks, depending on the species and on the weather. Robins may take from six to twenty days to build their nests, while field sparrows, which make very simple structures, often finish in two to four

Sooty Terns (*Sterna fuscata*)

Red-bellied Woodpecker (*Centurus carolinus*)

days. A blue jay in Florida may take longer to build its nest than the same species in Newfoundland, where the warm season is shorter. When birds have more than one brood during the same season, the second nest is usually built more quickly than the first.

Among passerine birds, both sexes often cooperate in building their nest on a site selected by the female, though sometimes the role of the male is simply that of cheerleader as he escorts the female, who searches for materials and carries them back to the nest. In species where no pair bond is formed, the female not only selects the nest site but does all the building herself; it is doubtful that the male even knows its location. Hummingbirds, grouse, woodcock, and ducks are some of the species that leave the work to the female. However, the male phalarope not only builds the nest and incubates the eggs after the female has deposited them; he alone cares for the young.

Obviously, each species has arrived at a different solution to meet the needs of its kind and the continuing changes in its environment. Not only have members of the same families, as among terns and owls, for instance, made very different solutions to their problems, but the success of each species that maintains a strong population proves the correctness of its way of doing things generation after generation.

Regardless of how long it takes to build the nest, whether it is built by both birds, built by the female alone, or by the male alone, it must be finished by the time the first egg is ready for laying. How these activities are synchronized is one of the continuing mysteries of bird biology.

The Egg

Familiar as we were from earliest childhood with hens' eggs in the kitchen, most of us looked at our first robin's nest with delight verging on incredulity. The blue-green eggs in it were lovely as jewels, and we had to be restrained from touching the enchanting fragile objects. No wonder the variety and beauty of birds' eggs have made them vulnerable in the past to collectors, whose greed brought some birds with particularly rare or coveted eggs dangerously close to extinction. Now in the United States it is illegal to take the eggs of any wild birds except under special government permits issued to scientists making particular studies.

In the great world of birds there is a tremendous variety of egg colors, ranging from blue, green, yellow, and occasionally purple to, rarely, dark red. Now and then an Australian emu has laid a completely black egg. Often eggs are decorated with spots, speckles, blotches, and streaks. The ground color is laid on first and then the markings, if any, are added to the egg as it moves through the oviduct. The pigment, especially the irregular streaks and spots, serves to camouflage those laid in the open. The scrawling streaks on a boat-tailed grackle egg, the spots on the egg of a spruce grouse, and the varied blotches and lines on those of a black skimmer help to conceal them in their natural environment. Loons that nest close to the shore of northern waters lay very dark, brownish-green spotted eggs that look enough like pebbles that they are seldom noticed unless the adult is seen as she slips off them into the water. Anybody who has walked near a least tern colony knows how difficult it is to see the eggs laid in plain sight on the sand. Hold one of these in your hand and you will be astonished by its conspicuous blotches on a whitish background. Put it gently back in the scrape nest and it becomes almost invisible.

Common murre eggs probably vary more in color than those of any other single species. Since they are laid on the bare rock, surely this helps each murre find its own egg on a ledge so crowded that each bird has little more than standing room. The eggs may be blotched or streaked or without any markings at all. Patterns may be black, various shades of brown, yellow, or red on a background of turquoise, red, ochre, cream, or white. In an experiment carried on in a murre colony in Europe it was found, when the eggs were moved about, that a murre would accept a strange egg only if it had a color and design similar to its own. Some murres are said to have reclaimed their own eggs when moved as much as twenty-five feet.

In contrast to the eggs of many colors and designs, whole families of birds lay white eggs. This is true of most birds that nest in holes, including woodpeckers. Their eggs do not require color for concealment. Some scientists believe the white eggs may actually help an adult, entering its dark hole, to find them. Owls, even those that nest in the open, have white eggs. These birds begin to incubate the first egg as soon as it is laid, so that camouflaging color is not needed. Critical to the protection of the eggs as color may be in many situations, almost all eggs become tarnished once incubation begins. Soiled plumage of the adult, rain, and the nesting materials contribute to this, though the colors of some eggs simply fade with age.

While round eggs are rare, those of owls are almost perfect spheres. Most plover eggs are broadly rounded at one end and bluntly pointed at the other so the four eggs (sometimes only three) fit neatly in the nest, pointed ends in the center with the rounded ends fanning out like the petals of a flower. The egg of a common murre is much more pointed than a plover egg, so it rolls safely in a circle if disturbed. The eggs of nighthawks and their relatives are long but almost equally rounded at either end.

The size of the egg itself is obviously controlled by

the size of the oviduct through which it must pass. Some members of the hummingbird family are the smallest birds in the world, so it is not surprising that they also lay the smallest eggs. A ruby-throated hummingbird's egg is about the size of a pea. The ostrich, the largest bird living today, lays the largest egg in the world. Weighing about three pounds, it equals from fifteen to eighteen hens' eggs, and you must allow forty minutes if you wish to hard-boil one of them. Measuring about one hundred and eight inches from tip to tip, the endangered California condor has the greatest wingspread of any North American bird. Every other year it lays the largest egg of any species on the continent, a single greenish-white one about four and three-tenths inches long. But the size of an egg is not always proportionate to the size of the bird that lays it. A ruddy duck lays eggs as large as those of a canvasback three times its size. The little ruddy duck weighs scarcely one pound, yet it has been known to lay as many as fourteen eggs with a total weight of three pounds. A tiny golden-crowned kinglet may lay eleven eggs that equal almost 125 percent of her weight. Few birds are as peculiar as the kiwis of New Zealand, so we should not be surprised that these birds outdo all other species by laying an egg weighing nearly a quarter of the weight of the female that lays it.

The majority of birds lay eggs with a shell that feels smooth to the touch, though some are glossy and others have a dull matte finish. South American great tinamous lay beautiful smooth green eggs that look and feel like the finest china. Chachalaca eggs have rough, almost corrugated shells. Duck eggs look and feel greasy and are water-resistant, while the eggs of an ani have a chalky surface that can be rubbed off. The shell of a white pelican egg resembles the uneven surface of a rock on which alternate freezing and heating have caused exfoliation. Both stork and ostrich eggs have a pitted surface.

A clutch is the number of eggs a bird lays for a single nesting. The size of the clutch varies greatly even within a given family. Hummingbirds and goatsuckers can be depended on to have two eggs in a clutch, but among boobies, a gannet has a clutch of one egg, while a blue-footed booby has two eggs. The clutch of many terns is variable, though a fairy tern has always one egg while a royal tern, which usually has two eggs, occasionally has as many as four. Generally, the clutch of a passerine bird will vary from three to five, but it is not unusual for a black-capped chickadee to have six or even eight eggs.

The trumpeter swan, the largest native waterfowl in North America, is said to lay as many as eight eggs, but I have never seen more than five in a clutch and, of these, usually only two or three hatched. Ducks are much smaller than swans, yet many species lay large clutches of ten or a dozen. Once on the Bear River

Clapper Rail (*Rallus longirostris*)

Refuge in Utah I found a gadwall nest with twenty-six eggs in it, the largest clutch I have ever seen. It is likely that two females laid in that nest.

Gallinaceous birds, often called upland game birds, may lay large clutches, but there is great variation. Several species of grouse lay about a dozen eggs, a ptarmigan seldom lays more than six, while bobwhites often lay fifteen. Ring-necked pheasants normally lay about a dozen eggs, but I have seen as many as twenty-two in a single nest.

No species, however, lays a larger clutch than it can cover adequately. Each species appears to have an instinctive knowledge of how many eggs should be in its nest and stops laying when that number is reached, though it is physically possible for some birds to lay many more eggs than they normally have in a clutch. For instance, E. H. Forbush in *Birds of Massachusetts* tells of a man who waited until a flicker laid two eggs in her nest, then removed one egg from it each time she added another. That flicker laid seventy-one eggs in seventy-three days while doing her best to achieve a clutch of six or eight eggs. If a clutch is destroyed, many birds build another nest and lay another clutch. This fact was put to use in former years when wild bird eggs were gathered for sale in cities. "Eggers" sailed to islands where gulls, terns, and other water birds nested and broke every egg they could find, then returned three or four days later and collected all the eggs, knowing they were fresh. It is said that more than three million murre eggs were sold in San Francisco alone over a six-year period for twenty cents or less per dozen.

Many species, however, having lost their eggs to a predator or other disaster, will not lay any more until the next season. Strangely enough, it is usually birds that lay only one or two eggs that do not lay again to replace lost clutches. Puffins lay but one egg annually and almost vanished from islands off the coast of Maine because so many of their eggs were taken for human food, a practice now forbidden by law.

Scientists suggest that the number of eggs normally laid in a clutch evolved through countless millennia until a stable population for the species was achieved. Birds that suffered the greatest annual losses, for whatever reason, laid many eggs, while those less affected by the hazards of life required fewer eggs to maintain their numbers at a satisfactory level. This natural system apparently worked very well until the human population began to explode, becoming a geological force and changing the world too rapidly for the slow process of evolutionary adaptation to function. The greatest disaster to birds has been the radical change and loss of habitat needed for nesting. Though of lesser consequence to bird populations, the annual mass killing of migrating birds that strike buildings, wires, television towers, and other obstacles in their path often makes people aware of the dangers birds face in a man-controlled world. On oceanic islands the introduction of dogs, cats, and especially rats has meant devastating predation where formerly there was little or none. The widespread use of pesticides, often carried to the most remote parts of the earth by winds, has been an important factor in the decline of birds. Today many species that normally lay few eggs are in danger of extinction. We are losing our magnificent whooping cranes, condors, eagles, and peregrines, and gaining instead a plethora of small birds: starlings, house sparrows, and blackbirds, species that not only have good-sized clutches but often two or more broods a season.

Many passerine birds and some birds of other orders lay an egg every day until the clutch is complete. Barn owls lay every second or third day. It takes a grouse about fifteen days to lay ten eggs. Birds most often lay their eggs in the morning, but this is by no means a fixed rule. Neither is the time of courtship and egg-laying always in the spring. In Florida great horned owls lay their eggs in late October or November. Sometimes bald eagles, which also nest there in the late autumn or early winter, return to their eyries only to find them occupied by great horned owls that started nesting a week or two earlier. The owl has such formidable talons that once it has seized an eagle nest, it is able to maintain possession and drive away its rightful owner. Brown pelicans have been found at some stage of their nesting cycle every month of the year. This is possible because they live in warm coastal regions of the south where ample food is available throughout the year. Snowy owls that nest on the far northern tundra face a very different situation. The hatching of their eggs must coincide with the period of greatest abundance of rodent life, especially lemmings, on which their young will be fed. When the rodents that go through a regular cycle of abundance and scarcity are at the top of their cycle, snowy owls may lay as many as eight eggs, but during years when the rodent population crashes, the owls may lay no more than four eggs and sometimes none at all.

Though cold can injure an egg, heat is much more dangerous to it. In hot places an adult must cover or shade its eggs to protect them from the sun from the moment the first one is laid until the clutch is complete. Shading the eggs, however, is not incubation, for they remain unchanged. Incubation begins when one or both parents tend the eggs regularly. Regularity is vital, for the eggs cannot develop without remaining almost continuously at a certain temperature—usually between 90 and 95 degrees F.

In spite of exceptions, the majority of eggs in the temperate zone are incubated during the mild days of spring and early summer when they are more susceptible to heat than to cold. Birds that begin to incubate their eggs as soon as the first one is laid, rather than waiting for the entire clutch, will hatch the eggs at intervals that may take several days or even a matter of weeks. This behavior is regular among owls and many raptors. The same is true of some passerine birds, including gray jays and Clark's nutcrackers, which nest during bitter weather toward the end of winter when snow still lies on the ground. If an owl or a hawk has a large clutch, the first chick to hatch may be almost ready to fledge by the time the last egg hatches. If there is a shortage of food, the smallest chicks in the nest may be devoured by their older siblings. Individual birds of the same species vary in attentiveness to the eggs, which can also affect their development. Sometimes there are differences from year to year in the length of time it takes gull eggs to hatch, and entire colonies are affected by whatever controls the period of incubation. Other birds, however, may not begin genuine incubation until the clutch is complete, so all the embryos begin to develop at once within the fertilized eggs and later all hatch at approximately the same time.

If both parents incubate the eggs, each bird will have a brood patch—that is, a bare area on the ventral surface of the body formed when the feathers and down fall out or are molted. The skin thickens, becoming spongy, and a concentration of blood vessels provides extra warmth. During incubation the feathers are parted and the parent shuffles the eggs about until all are brought into contact with the bare skin. Most passerine birds and many raptors have a single median brood patch. Puffins and shorebirds have two very small brood patches close to the thighs, while gulls, herons, and grouse are among the species that have three.

Since cold water touching the skin of a bird can lead to pneumonia, many water birds either have no brood

Least Tern (*Sterna albifrons*)

patch or a very small one, or, like the grebes, a slitlike patch that closes completely when the bird slips off the nest into the water. Male phalaropes, which do all the incubating of their eggs, not surprisingly have a brood patch while the females have none. Male and female gannets share incubation duties, but neither has a brood patch. They have solved the warmth problem in an interesting way through adaptation of their big webbed feet. One large foot is placed like a pancake over the chalky, stained egg, then the second foot is wrapped over the first, and the gannet lowers its body onto the nest. Large blood vessels in its feet warm the egg as efficiently as if it were covered with a heating pad.

Unlike most birds whose brood patches are created by molting, a natural part of their breeding cycle, ducks must create their own. As incubation time approaches, extra long down grows on the duck's breast and belly. She plucks this down to make a nest lining, often so ample it can be pulled completely over the eggs when she leaves the nest. In Iceland, common eiders have been practically domesticated for many decades. Harvesters take part of the down, which is used for clothing, bedding, and so forth, leaving enough so the eggs will not be harmed. Most eiders nest in a cold, foggy climate where the ample blanket of down, at once the lightest yet best insulating material in nature, protects the eggs from bitter cold. But whether ducks live in the cold north or in a warmer climate, all pull down from their bodies and add it to their nests. Hundreds of redheads nest on the flats of the Bear River Refuge in Utah, where the short grasses give them little protection from the blazing sun, which can quickly kill unprotected eggs. The insulating blanket of down that the redhead pulls over her eggs whenever she leaves the nest protects them from the heat as effectively as eider eggs are protected from the cold.

Male passerine birds are often very brightly colored, while the female is relatively drab and blends into the nest as inconspicuously as a leaf. Sensibly, she is the one who incubates the eggs. In the meantime, the male confines his activity to protecting the territory and to singing, occasionally feeding the female, and covering the nest for a brief time when his mate leaves for food or rest. The handsome black and white male rose-breasted grosbeaks, with a rosy triangle on the breast, surprisingly enough incubate the eggs with considerable regularity and often sing as they put in time on the eggs.

Among passerine birds, when both parents look alike they generally share incubation duties to some extent, if not equally. Blue jays, catbirds, and mockingbirds fall into this category. Male trumpeter swans and Canada geese look like the females, though they are larger than their mates, but they do not incubate the eggs. Instead, the cob and the gander stay near the nest to protect the pen and the goose, respectively. Both are strong fighters and fearless in protecting their mates and her eggs. Mute swan cobs, the heaviest of the roughly one hundred and forty-five species of waterfowl in the world, are even more aggressive in protecting their families. One man who attacked a mute swan pen as she incubated her eggs had his arm broken by the cob. There is a record in England of a cob that drowned a boy who beat a pen with a club as she cared for her eggs.

The drake does not help the duck build the nest or incubate the eggs. While the female is on the nest, he spends the time feeding, swimming with other drakes, or standing on a favored spot as far as a mile from his mate. In several species the drake appears to keep a watchful eye on the female, and when she leaves the nest to feed he may join her in her flight to water, swim about with her, then escort her back to the nest afterward. Drake eiders have been known to come to the rescue when a raven or gull attacked their incubating mates.

A female mourning dove incubates the eggs at night, then the male takes over for about an eight-hour shift during the day. Pileated woodpeckers reverse this, the male caring for the eggs at night and the female in the day. A male ostrich with a harem of several females, all of whom lay their eggs in a single place, does most of the incubation, with irregular help from his harem members. Many birds share incubation in rather short periods of three- or four-hour shifts. Both sexes of black-necked stilts, avocets, and double-crested cormorants exchange nest duties in this way.

Each time a bird returns to its eggs after a relief period, or when an exchange of duties between mates occurs, the eggs are turned. The bill is used for this essential task. It is believed that turning the eggs prevents adhesion of the embryo to the shell, and artificial incubators used to hatch domestic or wild bird eggs turn them mechanically at least three times every twenty-four hours. Yet in the South Pacific the palm swift, which builds one of the strangest of all nests by gluing some feathers to the underside of a palm frond, glues her two eggs to the top of the feathers as soon as they are laid, so turning them is impossible. Perhaps the ceaseless swaying of the large leaf to which the nest is attached serves the same purpose. The swift incubates her two eggs while clinging upright to her odd nest.

Apparently, incubating the eggs is a pleasant duty, for many a bird must be gently nudged off the eggs by a mate who wishes to take charge of them. The male black-necked stilt is particularly reluctant to surrender nest duties and often refuses to leave the first two or three times the female returns expecting to take over nest duties. When at last he consents to an exchange, it

is prefaced by a charming inspection of the eggs by both birds.

People who watch birds at their nests find the exchange ceremonies between partners who share incubation duties a most interesting phase of their behavior. A brown pelican approaches its nest with deliberate, ponderous steps, its great bill held vertically and its head waving from side to side. The mate on the nest bows deeply and lifts its wings. Both preen briefly and soon the relieved bird takes off. Snowy egrets share incubation, and their exchange ceremony is particularly attractive: the incubating bird recognizes its mate from a distance and stands on the nest, erecting all its delicate plumes. The returning bird responds by lifting its plumes and running gracefully along the limb that supports the nest or flying to it, if necessary, and often presents a stick, a gift which is accepted with enthusiasm and immediately tucked into the nest as the two birds join in a guttural chant.

Although some scientists have stated that Leach's petrel eggs hatch in forty-two days, it is generally accepted that their single white egg is incubated in from forty-eight to fifty-four days, the longest incubation period of any North American species. Both petrels care for their egg, but one stays with it for two or even three days while its mate feeds far out at sea. Their exchange takes place at night and is prefaced by musical warbling as one returns from feeding beyond sight of land. Its mate in the underground burrow answers with the same song. The duet ends with an exchange as the hungry petrel flies off into the night in search of food, while its well-fed mate pushes its small white egg close to its body and settles down quietly in the dark burrow.

Incubation periods vary from about eleven days, though occasionally house-sparrow eggs have hatched in ten days, to as long as eighty-two days for some wandering albatross eggs. The incubation period has little relation to the size of the species. Tiny ruby-throated hummingbirds incubate their eggs about sixteen days while the golden-crowned kinglet, scarcely larger than the hummingbird, hatches its eggs in only fourteen days. Warblers, sparrows, and robins have an average incubation period of twelve to fourteen days. A killdeer, the same size as a robin, incubates its eggs about twenty-six days, while a roseate spoonbill incubates its clutch from twenty-three to twenty-four days.

Barring disaster, the embryos within the eggs develop normally and hatching occurs at the end of a specific period. If this fails to happen on schedule, most birds remain on the eggs for three or four days before abandoning them. Occasionally, the time clock of an individual bird goes awry and, though the eggs are infertile or do not hatch for some other reason, the bird keeps right on incubating them. A determined ruffed grouse was once recorded as having incubated

Killdeers (*Charadrius vociferus*)

and debris into a great pile as much as eight feet high and twenty-four feet in circumference. Rains wet this pile and, as fermentation takes place, the rotting debris heats up. When the female is ready to lay an egg, a chamber is dug in the pile and the egg is deposited in it and covered. It may be several days before she returns to lay another egg, and this leisurely laying procedure may go on for weeks. The male repeatedly tests the temperature of the pile. When it climbs toward 100 degrees F. he pulls away some of the material, and if it falls below the upper 80s, he adds to the pile. After sixty-three days or more have passed, a little mallee fowl is hatched and digs its way to the surface without help. By that time its feathers are sufficiently developed so that it can actually fly a few yards. If a young megapode ever meets its parents, they do not know each other, for the small bird is self-reliant from the moment it scrambles out of its birthplace, which in many ways resembles a compost pile.

While we enjoy the first days of summer, at the opposite end of the earth the Antarctic winter is beginning. That is the time when emperor penguins assemble on the icy southern continent to breed. In due time the females each lay a single egg. A male immediately rolls the egg onto his large webbed feet and covers it with a pouchlike fold of skin. He must be quick about this or another male, lacking an egg, will steal it from him. Once the females have each laid an egg, they begin their journey to the open sea, where they will rest and feed for two months. In the meantime each male, having adjusted his egg satisfactorily, huddles close to his fellows, for these penguins do not build nests. There they stand patiently without eating, each holding his egg, for two long months in the most severe climate in the world, where snow sometimes almost buries them and the temperature dips to 40 degrees or more below zero. If the female does not return on time, the male still has enough reserve to give his chick one feeding when it breaks out of the shell at the end of sixty to sixty-four days. If his mate fails to return, perhaps having been eaten by a leopard seal, the young penguin will die of starvation. But, as if spurred by an alarm clock, most female emperor penguins actually return at the precise time when they are needed by their thin, exhausted mates and their hungry chicks. They arrive sleek and rested, ready to take over the care of the young penguins.

its eggs for seventy days, though the normal period is twenty-three to twenty-four days. Incubation time for bobwhite eggs is the same as for its relative, the ruffed grouse, yet one stayed on its eggs for three months. On the other hand, some individuals are so inflexibly ruled by their instincts that they abandon live eggs two or three days short of hatching.

Incubation may be lengthened or shortened by cold or by heat, by rain or by drought, and by other weather influences, including wind. Wind may be helpful when it is very hot, but harmful when temperatures plummet.

Some birds have extremely strange nesting habits. Egyptian plovers live along sandy river banks in North Africa and habitually take advantage of solar heat to help care for their eggs. The coursers brood the eggs at night, but it does not take the morning sun long to pour down so much heat that it becomes very hot indeed. Then the coursers bury their eggs in the sun-heated sand and incubation goes forward without attention from the parents. In Australia and its adjacent islands there is an unusual family of birds known as megapodes. One of these, the mallee fowl, is about the size of a domestic hen. The male, sometimes helped by the female, spends most of the year scraping leaves

Hatching

We have mentioned some of the variations in size, color, and pattern of birds' eggs but little about the egg itself, which, as Shakespeare rightly put it, is full of meat. When laid, the shell is largely filled with food materials, but a thin disk of protoplasm lies on the surface of the yolk. This weighs very little and as the egg is turned it turns also, so that it is always on top. Though the egg has been fertilized, nothing happens until incubation begins, but as soon as this is initiated, development takes place rapidly. In a domestic hen's egg, a heart is formed in the amorphous mass and begins to beat in only thirty-six hours. Food flows from the yolk to the growing embryo and the astonishing speed of development continues unabated. By the end of forty-eight hours many of the organs—brain, ears, and eyes—have taken on definite shape.

As this amazing development takes place, the embryo, curled inside the shell, is attached to the yolk, which supplies most of its food. The egg white is used to a lesser extent for nourishment and, to aid in building the skeleton, a small amount of calcium is absorbed from the shell, weakening it slightly. This weakening is surely helpful when the difficult task of hatching begins. It must have been of particular importance to the embryo of the now extinct elephant bird of Madagascar. The thick-walled, heavy shells of those eggs, the largest ever discovered, are known only from a few used as containers by the natives or found in the swamps of that large island. One of these eggs, six times the size of an ostrich egg, will hold two gallons of water. A mathematically minded scientist has estimated that one of these would hold the contents of thirty-three thousand vervain hummingbird eggs. Since the shells were much stronger than clay pots, no wonder the natives of Madagascar used them as bowls and for storing food and water whenever they were fortunate enough to find them. The last of these ten-foot-tall, quarter-ton birds survived into the seventeenth century, well after Magellan made the first trip around the world.

As the embryo grows, the yolk shrinks and the air space at the large end of the egg expands, so by the time the embryo has completed its development the air chamber occupies almost a quarter of the shell. A day or two before the egg hatches, the embryo, with its head turned toward the larger, rounded end of the egg, pushes its bill through the membrane into the air chamber and immediately begins to breathe. Some species, especially gallinaceous birds, begin to cheep softly at this time. The yolk sac still contains anywhere from a third to a seventh of its original bulk; this is a reserve food supply that will see the young bird through the first hours—and in some species the first several days—of its life. The yolk sac is extremely fragile. A person thinking he will help the bird as it struggles to get out of the shell usually causes this to rupture, and he kills the bird with mistaken kindness.

Apparently, once the air chamber is punctured, the parents are aware of the momentous happening in their nest, perhaps because they hear a faint cheeping. Certainly they must feel the struggle of the young bird as it proceeds with the task of opening the shell. Should the parents give an alarm call at this stage, the embryo instantly becomes quiet. Already it is instinctively reacting to the outside world and understands the meaning of its parents' signals.

Though the shell has weakened during incubation, the hatching process is a very difficult one. Some species, perhaps most, are provided by nature with a strong hatching muscle in the neck, and though birds do not have teeth in the usual sense, most embryos are provided with a tool called an egg tooth, a small, rough, triangular growth near the tip of the upper mandible. The embryo uses its hatching muscle and the egg tooth as its instruments of escape from the imprisoning shell. After hatching is complete, the muscle shrivels away and the equally transitory egg tooth falls off, for they are of no further use.

As soon as the embryo begins to breathe, its neck muscle pushes the egg tooth so strongly against the shell that a star-shaped crack is made. Then, moving with a circular progression inside the blunt end of the egg, the tooth probes and files to widen the crack, until finally the bill breaks through. At last the egg is pipped. The opening slowly widens as the embryo stretches and moves rhythmically. With some species, piece after piece of shell falls away, while in others a series of perforations is made until finally the entire top of the egg breaks away like a cap. The struggle is exhausting and the embryo often stops to rest, for the labor may take anywhere from a few hours to two days or more. Freedom comes suddenly. Wet and exhausted, the hatchling lies limp and quiet for a few minutes. It is no longer an embryo. It is now a bird.

While hatching takes place, the parent birds behave in various ways. Blue jays are normally very shy when incubating, yet when the eggs are hatching they become courageous and refuse to leave the nest even when danger threatens. A shorebird may stay on the eggs at that time while its mate displays its "broken wing" act, feigning an injury that frequently succeeds in drawing a predator away from the nest. I once lifted an adult marbled godwit off her nest after one of her four eggs had hatched to see how the pipped eggs were progressing. At any other time a godwit will be up and away, screaming frantically, even when I am still a hundred feet away from the nest and my photography

Black Skimmers (*Rynchops niger*)

blind. Mockingbirds sometimes stand on the rim of their nests and sing as the eggs hatch, and cranes, too, are especially solicitous during the hatching period. The pair stands beside or on the nest regarding the eggs, sometimes touching them, and making sounds that seem for all the world like a parental consultation.

Observers have found that about a third of all eggs hatch at night and about half in the morning hours, while the smallest number hatch in the afternoon.

Some incubating birds signal to their mates when hatching is imminent, and this triggers an immediate shift from incubating behavior to feeding behavior. The male cedar waxwing is assiduous in his attention to the female as she spends about two weeks incubating the eggs, frequently taking berries to the nest for her. When she signals the news that the eggs are hatching, he may display a premature burst of feeding behavior and bring caterpillars to the nest before the helpless baby waxwings are ready to eat.

All hatchlings are wet and weary when at last they have broken away the top of the shell and kicked themselves free. Most of them are brooded at least until the initial moisture dries. But from that moment on, the lives of the baby birds take dramatically contrasting paths. Some are called precocial birds, others altricial birds.

When a precocial bird hatches its eyes are open, it is covered with down, and it is strong enough to run about as soon as it is dry. Most precocial birds have a longer incubation period in a larger egg than altricial birds that are the same size when mature. The added time in the shell enables them to develop more completely.

Once precocial birds leave the nest, they never return, yet from time to time the young birds are called together and brooded by one of the parent birds. Since their body-temperature regulators are not firmly established until they are several days old, a sudden drop in temperature or a rainstorm at this critical time may be fatal. So far as we know, only the young precocial megapode has a well-regulated temperature control at the time it breaks out of its egg.

Because the majority of young precocial birds leave the nest soon after hatching, it is vital that the entire clutch hatch at the same time. Ducks, grouse, and shorebirds lead their young from the nest within a few hours after hatching, and unhatched eggs are abandoned even though the embryos may still be alive. If incubation had been continued a few more hours these would have hatched, but left behind they are doomed. This may seem a heartless waste of life, but predators attracted to the nest by the process of hatching could end the life of the entire clutch instead of one or two unhatched eggs. The empty shells and any eggs that fail to hatch on time are simply left behind. There is often a strong odor accompanying hatching, and though most birds have little or no sense of smell, they know instinctively that they must leave the discarded egg shells speedily before a predator with an acute sense of smell finds the hidden nest. Moreover, the egg shells, camouflaged before hatching, now become conspicuous as their white lining becomes visible.

Goslings huddle under the goose until they are dry and may remain there for several hours or even a day or two. In that snug darkness they rub against her plumage, and their yellow down becomes oiled and water-proofed. When ready to leave the nest, they follow her to the water, usually escorted by the gander, who takes an active part in protecting the young family.

The female ruffed grouse is never helped by her mate either in building or defense of the nest, which is usually placed beside a fallen log or close to a tree trunk. She incubates the eggs alone for more than three weeks, her mottled brown plumage and immobile form rendering her almost invisible among last year's dead leaves. The eggs hatch almost simultaneously, and within a brief time the downy brown young follow their mother away from the nest. Spotted sandpipers are well-known shorebirds, but this name is sometimes deceptive, for they may nest almost to tree line on damp mountain slopes. Their four dark, speckled eggs are incubated from twenty to twenty-four days, mostly by the male. As soon as the young are dry, they become active and the male leads them away, perhaps assisted by the female. Though they are only an inch and a half long when hatched, the tiny sandpipers teeter on their long spindly legs exactly as their parents do.

When an altricial bird breaks out of the shell it is as wet and exhausted as a precocial bird, but instead of becoming a charming ball of fluffy down when dry, it looks like a wriggling, unformed bit of pink protoplasm. Most are naked, though some species have a few tufts of down that only serve to emphasize their undressed bodies. Their delicate skin is so transparent that some of the viscera are visible. The big head and the closed, swollen blind eyes are monstrous in proportion to shoulders and chest. The large abdomen bulges and the thin neck looks far too fragile to hold the head.

Unlike the precocial birds, which lead their young away from the nest, where the hatched eggs have become conspicuous, the altricial bird carries the shells away and drops them some distance from the nest, or she may smash the shells and swallow them. It is not clear if this has any nutritional function, but in any case, it is an efficient disposal system. Among flamingos, the young themselves eat the shells, in which they have been enclosed from twenty-eight to thirty-two days.

Because of their vulnerability, most altricial birds must be brooded almost constantly for the first few days, but they grow very rapidly, as we shall see in the following chapter. In a matter of days blackish-gray hatchling gannets are covered with woolly white down and herons with long fluffy down, while songbirds still show areas of bare skin even after the still-sheathed flight features have pushed through the skin.

Songbird chicks grow rapidly. By the time they are four days old they can be left alone for brief periods in mild weather. By the time they are eight to ten days old, their temperature-control system is stabilized. This is an important milestone in their lives, though even with an efficient internal thermostat, their temperature may vary during any twenty-four-hour period. The normal temperature is always lowest among primitive birds and highest among the most highly developed species. That of the kiwi is about 100 degrees F., while that of the song thrush of Europe has been recorded at 111.6 degrees F.

Both the spotted sandpiper and the Baltimore oriole measure seven and a half inches in length, but the former is precocial and the latter altricial. By comparing them, we see the sharp contrast between these two types of birds. A spotted sandpiper egg must be incubated from twenty to twenty-four days before the young bird breaks the shell and thrusts it aside. As quickly as the bird dries off it can run about and even climb on the back of its parent as incubation of the unhatched eggs continues. As soon as the last (fourth) egg has hatched and the young are all dry, they are led from the nest and begin to feed on their own, following the example of their parents. The eggs of the oriole are smaller than those of the sandpiper and are incubated only twelve to fourteen days. The newly hatched orioles are completely helpless, unable to do anything but hold up their heads and beg for food. They must remain in their hanging nest for about two weeks before they are strong enough to leave it. Even then they are not on their own, but depend on their parents to supply them with food for several more days.

Not all birds that come from large eggs incubated for a long time are precocial. A white pelican has a huge three-and-a-half inch egg that is incubated for about thirty-six days. A gannet's egg is half an inch shorter, but it must be incubated for about forty-two days. Both white pelican and gannet young are blind and helpless when hatched, for in spite of the large size of the eggs and the long incubation period, they are altricial birds.

It is not easy to place all birds in perfectly defined categories, for we are always finding exceptions. The Leach's storm-petrel is one of the altricial misfits. This eight-inch petrel lays an egg about the size of a robin's, but instead of hatching in about thirteen days as a robin's egg does, it requires fifty-four days, the longest incubation period of any North American species.

When hatched in its dark burrow on an oceanic island, the tiny bird is covered with dense black down and its eyes are open. Though altricial, it looks like a precocial bird, but it must remain in the burrow for about forty days, where it is fed by both parents and grows extremely fat. Then the adults desert the chick and it stays on in the burrow without food for twenty or thirty days more, growing feathers and losing weight steadily as its fat is used to nourish its body. Finally, when sixty or seventy days old, it moves at night to the mouth of the burrow and, on untried wings, flies strongly off to sea, where it will remain beyond sight of land for two years or more until it is mature enough to breed. Common puffins with a rather similar youthful story are precocial birds. They remain in the nest from forty-five to fifty-six days, but the adults stop feeding them during the last few days they remain in the nest cavity. Finally, one night the young puffin walks to the edge of the island and, with fluttering wings, drops into the ocean it has never seen. Immediately it begins to swim in the direction of open water, and to dive and fish as skillfully as it swims. How long it is before these chunky little birds that take to the water so expertly are able to fly is not known. Once they travel beyond sight of land their lives are largely shrouded in mystery until they are at least two years old, when some of them, still too young to breed, return to the vicinity of the island where they spent their early days. They do not breed before they are three years old, perhaps older.

It is easy for amateur bird-watchers to separate the blind, helpless young altricial birds from precocial birds born covered with down and able to run about, leaving the nest almost at once. But the intermediates are confusing. Petrels and puffins are among the birds that fall into this class. It must be remembered that man, for his convenience, has arranged all organisms in groups that have some common factors. Nature, always experimenting, offers many exceptions, and cannot be made to fit perfectly within fixed, man-made rules. We find exceptions in almost every classification man makes. These exceptions may puzzle us, but they add a depth of interest to our observations of the working of nature.

The Growing Family

Young birds have been called "eating machines" and their bright mouths "food targets." We shall soon see the truth of these terms, for some birds eat their weight in food during the period of greatest growth, and their gaily colored mouths held invitingly open stir their parents to ever greater efforts to satisfy their enormous hunger. Almost all birds are given animal food of some kind in the beginning. Only later do the seed- and fruit-eating birds graduate to the varied food on which they will depend as adults. Ravenous as growing birds may be, their hunger is not aroused immediately after hatching. The lull before hunger awakens may be only hours, while among some birds a few days may go by before food is needed. A part of the egg yolk remains in the belly of many young birds to nourish them after they hatch, though the amount varies with each species. Nearly half the yolk may be present when a swan cygnet or a diving duck hatches, enough to see it through the first days of life without additional food. This is true of domestic chickens and explains why those shipped from a hatchery need not be fed during two or three days of travel; remaining egg yolk takes care of their food needs until the farmer receives them. When they are three or four days old and are offered chick-feed, the infant birds, never having known a parent because they were hatched in an incubator, know instinctively how to feed themselves.

Most upland game birds retain about 35 percent of the yolk when hatched. A mother pheasant or grouse quickly leads her young away from the nest, but she makes no attempt to feed them. No doubt her young family watches as she picks up tidbits, and she may even indicate that certain objects are good to eat or pick up an insect and drop it in front of a young bird. But she never feeds them directly. By the time the egg yolk is exhausted, the chicks know how to feed themselves.

Many young precocial birds give the impression that they are eager to begin life away from the nest while others seem reluctant to leave. The young spotted sandpiper that hatched and dried off before its three nest-mates (pages 98–99) was not content to remain quietly in the nest until its siblings were ready to leave, but climbed over the incubating parent. A clutch of goose eggs, however, may be about the size of a spotted sandpiper clutch and hatch as irregularly, but the first goslings to break out of their eggs huddle quietly under the goose while the remaining eggs hatch, and all may stay in the nest for as long as two days before leaving their dark, warm shelter.

Altricial birds exhaust most of the egg yolk by the time they are hatched and must be fed within a few hours while being continuously brooded. The hatching itself probably triggers the change from incubation behavior to feeding behavior in the adults. When food is brought to the nest the heads of all the helpless little birds shoot up and begin to wave about, in spite of their fragile-looking necks. The mouths, with brightly colored flanges, are surprisingly large for such small creatures and all open wide to receive food.

As we have seen, every species has its own code of signals essential for courtship and the formation of the pair; without the correct signals the birds cannot mate. Signals of a different kind are just as vital to the survival of the young birds, who must indicate to their parents when they are hungry and where to put the food. Many altricial birds, especially songbirds, have brightly colored bills that will fade once they are old enough to care for themselves. White, cream, or yellow skin usually surrounds the gape so that when the bill is opened the inside of the huge mouth looks rather like a bright, diamond-shaped flower. Striking colors line the mouth and point the way to the throat, where food must be placed or the nestling cannot swallow it.

Anybody who has ever acted as foster parent to a baby crow knows that putting food near the tip of the bill is useless; it must be pushed deep into the throat until you feel the strong pull of the muscles there as the food is sucked down.

The vivid mouth lining of some horned larks is emphasized by black dots that point the way down, and a few birds have beadlike structures that seem to glow, especially useful in dark nests. House sparrows have tiny knobs in the mouth that reflect light, and a young meadowlark has white hairlike growths on the roof of the mouth that point toward the throat, like the hairs of a pitcherplant leaf. Two large, white-edged projections in the lower jaw seem to say, "Put it here."

No matter what color the mouth lining of the baby birds (red, orange, or yellow, or a combination of these colors), or what the added decorations (black, white, blue, green, purple, or opalescent), the sight arouses frantic efforts by the parents. We know that these are special targets to aid the parents in feeding their young because as soon as the youngsters can feed themselves, the bright colors fade and the decorations vanish. In addition to color signals, songbird nestlings attract the attention of their food-bearing parents by stretching their necks as far as they can, quivering their heads, and cheeping furiously.

A female robin incubates her eggs alone, but as soon as they hatch, a deep-seated instinct to feed them is aroused in the male. He stops singing and defending his territory to join his mate in collecting food for the hatchlings. Visits to the nest by both parents follow one another quickly; sometimes both arrive at the same time, each with a bill crammed with earthworms, which are stuffed into the gaping mouths.

A helpless infant robin develops quickly. By the third day its blind eyes begin to open, and at five days it can turn in the nest to face its parents as they arrive with food. When seven days old it exercises legs and wings, and at ten days it preens the unsheathed feathers that began to push through the skin at four days of age. It begins to peck at objects in the nest and sometimes at its nest siblings. By the time the robins are thirteen days old and ready to leave the nest, their birth weight has multiplied many times over. It has been estimated that a young robin can eat fourteen feet of earthworms in a single day. Anyone who has tried to find some earthworms for fishing on a late spring day wonders how the robins find enough of them to cope with the insatiable hunger of four or five demanding nestlings. By the end of two weeks, a robin chick will manage a weak, fluttering flight away from the nest. In those few short days it has changed from a tiny, helpless infant into a bird as heavy as its parents.

We know that birds have the highest metabolism of any creatures in the world and require a great deal of food just to survive. Baby birds must grow rapidly. The chicks of many species eat their own weight in food each day. Because of the enormous amount of food required, young birds usually hatch at a time when food is most abundant; swarms of midges, damselflies, mosquitoes, and other insects often coincide with the arrival of chicks, as does the appearance of seeds, berries, and other fruits. We rarely consider in concrete terms the amount of food young birds consume. Dr. Niko Tinbergen, after studying a large gull colony off the coast of Britain, estimated that at the height of the season in a gull colony of approximately forty-eight thousand growing gulls, about twenty tons of food were transported to the island daily, or almost a pound for each young gull. Often the amounts fed are small, but the frequency of feeding is high. When barn swallows are eight days old they are fed about once a minute. House wrens have fed their young 491 times a day, while phoebes have been known to take food to their young a grand total of 845 times in a single day. It is no surprise that many passerine birds grow so rapidly!

A California condor, however, seldom feeds its single young more than twice a day, and it grows so slowly that it must remain in the nest for four to five months. Golden eagles feed their young only three or four times a day. Both these raptors range widely to find the prey to take to the nest, but probably no bird in the world flies so far to find the needed food as the wandering albatross. Bands attached to their legs prove

Wood Thrushes (*Hylocichla mustelina*)

that these adults will travel up to twenty-five hundred miles from their nests to find food for their slow-growing, infrequently fed, single chicks. White pelicans are tiny and helpless at hatching, but by the time they are sixty days old they weigh from three to five pounds more than their sixteen-pound parents. This surplus weight must be lost before they can make a genuine flight.

Raptors, such as hawks, eagles, and owls, catch their food in their talons and use these same talons to carry the food to the nest. Red-tailed hawks appear to be especially fond of snakes; it is not uncommon to see one of them flying heavily with a large black snake dangling below like the mooring of a balloon. Black snakes eat many young birds; then, in turn, they become food for other nestlings. At first, predatory birds tear their prey apart and place bits in the mouths of the young, but later on, the prey is simply dropped on the nest and the young must tear it apart themselves. The hummingbird female carries nothing visible to the nest, but her crop is filled with nectar and tiny insects. The two young hummingbirds, aware of her approach, open their slender bills wide and she thrusts her bill inside one of the gaping mouths and begins to jab up and down. It is an alarming sight, for it seems certain that she will kill her delicate young. Though her actions appear savage and even deadly, her method of feeding is effective. Gorged at last, the chicks subside and sleep off the nutritious meal. Many other species also carry the food in their crops or gizzards. Cedar waxwings can do this without damaging the fruit, but more often food carried this way is partly or even entirely digested by the parents when their babies are very young.

Murres and puffins are among the birds that actually fly under water, using their wings to propel themselves as they pursue fish. Puffins often catch several fish before returning to feed their young. Nobody can watch a puffin fly in from the sea to its nest with five or six fish dangling from its bill without wondering how it holds the first fish while catching the others. An anhinga swims after its prey, spears it with its sharp bill, then rises to the surface, flips off the fish, and catches it head-first in its mouth before taking it to the nest.

Colonial birds must leave their territories to collect food for their young. A gannet flies over the ocean in search of schools of fish and when a school is sighted, it may plunge from a height so great that the dive carries it as much as fifty feet beneath the surface.

Brown pelicans also dive for fish. They will often set out in groups from their nests, skimming the waves in long lines until they reach a satisfactory fishing area. Then they rise high in the air, where they can scan the water, then plunge when they sight suitable prey. Unlike brown pelicans, white pelicans fish from the surface and are among the few species of birds that cooperate in getting food. Several form a compact line and drive the fish before them until the fish become excited and begin to flip about, at which point the pelicans easily scoop them into their huge pouches. They do not carry the fish to their nestlings in the pouch, however, but in the crop where the catch is partly digested before being regurgitated for the young. At first the digested fish is dribbled to the tip of the bill, where the tiny nestlings can reach it. As the chicks grow bigger, they reach like impatient gluttons into the crop itself.

Swifts, nighthawks, swallows, and the aptly named flycatchers catch flying insects for their young as well as for themselves. The flycatchers perch on a branch, then dart out when an appetizing insect appears, but the other species chase the insects and scoop them into their large open mouths. It is claimed that some swifts, also aptly named, have been clocked at speeds up to two hundred miles an hour. Surely few insects sighted by these birds can escape pursuit. These insect eaters have tiny, weak bills, but their huge mouths make capacious carriers for their catch. They often travel a long distance to find an abundance of flying insects, but once they have discovered a concentration, they cram their mouths to the limit before returning to feed their young. Swallows make their insect catches in the daytime, while goatsuckers usually hunt for their nestlings at dawn and dusk, spending the bright hours brooding their young or simply resting.

Western Grebes (*Aechmophorus occidentalis*)

43

It seems evident that almost any type of plant or animal life can be exploited by some species of bird. Each is equipped by nature with the proper tools and techniques for obtaining its particular food. Everglade kites and limpkins, for example, specialize in collecting snails. The upper mandible of an Everglade kite extends into a long hook that is an efficient tool for extracting the snail from its shell. Not until Fred Truslow photographed the sequence did we know exactly how a limpkin, lacking any such tool, was able to remove the snail so efficiently. It took him more than two weeks to condition one limpkin so that he could stay close enough to it to photograph the process.

Few birds in all the world have as strange a method of finding food for their young as do oilbirds. During the daytime the birds remain on their nests in dark caves, but at night all is changed. The oilbirds sally forth to collect food, guided through the darkness by echoes of high-pitched calls like metallic clicks having a frequency of about seven thousand cycles a second. The sounds made by bats for their sonarlike guidance is beyond the range of human ears, but if we concen-trate, we can hear the oilbirds. They may travel as far as fifty miles to a food source. They are partial to certain rich, oily palm fruits which they pick while in full flight and swallow whole. Unlike the majority of birds, oilbirds have a well-developed sense of smell, which may help them to locate the pungent fruits that are later fed to the young by regurgitation. Oilbird chicks grow slowly but become enormously fat. By the time they are ten weeks old they weigh half again as much as their parents. Even though the Indians of Venezuela believed these birds were the souls of their ancestors condemned to live deep in dark caverns, they formerly gathered the young oilbirds and used their fat for cooking and for burning in their lamps.

Though many species, including goatsuckers, feed in the dim light of dusk and dawn, relatively few feed at night as oilbirds do unless there is a bright moon. Some owls are regular night feeders, however. A barn owl can follow and pounce on a scurrying mouse or rat in total darkness. It cannot see its prey and has no sonar guidance; only its acute hearing alerts it to the evasive tactics of the prey as it attempts to escape.

Canada Geese (*Branta canadensis*)

When the young in a heron colony hatch, there is great activity, for the young birds keep up a perpetual hunger cry and parents are constantly arriving with food and departing for more. You will never see any food in the claw or bill of a returning heron, for the catch of frogs, fish, small snakes, crustaceans, or even small mammals such as mice is carried in the crop. Though it may appear that the parent has returned without food, the young birds know better and the adult is greeted with loud cries, deep bows, and a frantic waving of heads. Finally one young heron seizes its parent's bill in a scissors hold and begins to tug. Slowly the food is regurgitated into the bill of the eager youngster. All young herons—from the goliath heron to the least bittern—feed by grasping the bill of the parent quite near its base with their own, and taking the fish or other food as it is returned from the crop to the mouth.

When the multitude of ravenous young California gulls clamor for food at the Bear River Refuge in Utah, it is sometimes difficult for the parents to satisfy their demands, particularly if they have a family of four or five. I have watched these gulls hunt in pairs the way cheetahs stalk their prey on the Serengeti Plains of East Africa. The pair search the open water until they locate a family of coots or a group of ducklings far from shore and a safe refuge among the rushes. Weaving back and forth, they circle above the family until the frightened birds are in a panic; then one gull swoops down and swallows a baby coot or duckling, then the second gull scoops up another baby bird. Having made a successful raid on helpless young birds, the gulls return to feed their hungry young.

When the California gulls reach their nests, they stand quietly. Near the tip of the lower mandible of each adult is a bright red spot that attracts the young gulls, who reach up and begin nibbling at it, becoming steadily more excited as they do so. First one parent and then the other responds to the ardent begging and coughs up its semidigested catch, which has turned into a dark, ball-like mass on which the young gulls feed. Except when it is difficult to find enough food for the demanding youngsters, the adult gulls search the shore for edible material washed up by the waves and insects from the water, pastures, and meadows.

Black skimmers, with their oddly shaped bills, feed in a unique manner. Often paralleling the curves of the shoreline, they fly so close to the water that the longer, under mandible cuts it like the blade of a pair of shears. After flying a few hundred feet, the skimmer reverses its flight, going back the way it came and catching little minnows attracted to the surface by the curious disturbance of the water made on the first flight. Like many young birds, baby skimmers do not eat for a time after hatching, but soon they accept eagerly the small fish dangling from their parents' bills

and swallow them whole. Sometimes skimmers and other parent birds misjudge the capacity of their newly hatched infants and offer them food far too large for the little birds to swallow. Then the parent takes it back and eats it.

For the first few days of their lives all birds of the dove family are fed "pigeon milk." During incubation there is a gradual thickening of the walls of the gizzard of both sexes, and by the time a young pigeon is ready for its first feeding, the gizzard walls of the parents have sloughed off into a thick, creamy substance as rich in protein, fat, and minerals as rabbit's milk. The young pigeon thrusts its bill deep into the mouth of either parent to drink this delectable food. As the squabs grow older, seeds are first softened in the gizzards of their parents and added to their diet.

Goldfinches also collect seeds that are partly digested in the crop, then regurgitated into the mouths of their young. All four or five nestlings are fed at each visit. Waxwings regurgitate food as well. It is amusing to watch a waxwing come to a nest where all the young birds are gaping widely. With a jerk and a gulp, up comes a berry or a chokeberry, and into a tiny throat it goes. One after another, a cherry appears as if by magic in the bill of the waxwing and is popped into a gaping mouth. Each young waxwing receives a cherry in turn. Sometimes the parent has stuffed so much food in its crop that each has a second round.

When the arrival of the parent is greeted by several open mouths, what determines which one shall receive the food if only one can be fed at a time? Usually the hungriest one makes the biggest fuss and begs the hardest. Into that demanding mouth goes the food. The stuffed nestling then subsides and perhaps goes to sleep, so that, at the next feeding, which may be made within five minutes, the next most eager baby is fed, and so on until the first is starving again and making urgent demands for food.

Woodpeckers collect most of their food from trees by probing for beetles, grubs, or insects in the bark and wood. At first young woodpeckers are fed in the bottom of the nest cavity, but after a few days they are strong enough to climb to the entrance, where the bird that plugs the hole is fed and keeps right on accepting food until it is pushed aside by another vigorously demanding sibling. The system is one of rotation, which works perfectly unless one is a weakling. That one rarely survives very long.

A swift makes about one visit an hour to the nest, but it arrives with its throat and crop packed with anywhere from one hundred to eight hundred insects, enough so that all the young birds in the nest can be fed at each visit. It is an interesting fact that when storms make flying insects disappear, the adults and young become torpid and do not feed. While summer storms rarely last many days, it has been reported that swifts have survived in a torpid state for up to three weeks. Many species become torpid in cold or stormy weather and their body temperatures drop sharply. This may also happen at night, when birds are simply enjoying normal sleep. Hummingbirds with excessively high metabolism eat more than three hundred times a day, consuming so many calories that they correspond to a human intake of one hundred and forty pounds of bread. To avoid starvation at night, their metabolism drops sharply to a level only one-fifteenth of its daytime rate, while their temperature drops to about 75 degrees F., enabling their bodies to stretch their store of food until dawn.

Brooding the very young birds and feeding the nestlings are by no means the only responsibilities of parent birds. The chicks must be protected, especially from ravenous predators that, like the young birds, must eat to live. When a ruffed grouse suspects danger, she gives a sharp vocal signal to the young, then explodes into the air with a startling report. As if by magic, the young vanish as they become motionless. Their cryptic colors and disruptive patterns blend harmoniously with the forest floor. If the intruder lingers, the grouse settles nearby and goes into an injury-feigning act, crying pitifully as she tries to coax a predator away from her family. A female grouse must protect her young alone, as must all birds in which a pair bond is not formed. Female gallinaceous birds, hummingbirds, and woodcock do all the work and care for their young without help from the male.

People who have visited tern colonies are often dived at and sometimes hit on the head by frantic birds, all shouting wild imprecations. Gulls are less likely to hit an intruder, but I have had great black-backed gulls strike me so hard on the head when I

came too near the nest that tears shot out of my eyes. Long-billed curlews, screaming loudly, often threaten attack, then swerve away without actually striking. Some birds are so dedicated to the defense of their young that they have severely injured people who threatened them. A great horned owl once destroyed the eye of a man who climbed to its nest. For many years there was a peregrine eyrie on the ledge of a mountain in Massachusetts from which the tercel, smaller than his mate, dashed out to give battle to everyone who attempted the climb to the nest. In a flashing stoop, the tercel would hit the intruder on the head with his closed fist, often causing painful, though not permanent, injuries. Even a friendly, mild-mannered catbird in a garden will fight, sometimes drawing blood, when defending its young held gently in the hand while a band is attached to its leg.

Farmers regard kingbirds nesting near their chicken yards as friends, for these small, aggressive flycatchers will attack any hawk that comes too near its territory, and while protecting their own nests, they also protect the chickens. Red-winged blackbirds seem timid and ready to flee from danger, yet when they have young many of them become very brave. I have watched a male red-wing attack a magpie that came near its nest, bouncing up and down over the magpie's back and pecking it so furiously that the large bird made a hasty retreat.

When a large family occupies a small nest, scrupulous sanitation seems essential to the health of the nestlings. Most songbird nests, when abandoned, are as clean as a baby's crib. Because these young birds defecate immediately after eating, the parents combine feeding with nest cleaning. Since the fecal sac is wrapped in a tough membrane, this is easily disposed of; some birds swallow it, perhaps for the undigested nutrients remaining in it. Later, as the young birds develop, this method of disposal stops; instead, the fecal sac is seized and carried off, then dropped haphazardly away from the nest. Collected in the nest, the fecal matter would attract insects; around the edge it would attract predators. Yet among some birds, once the young are about two-thirds grown, the feces is no longer removed by the parents.

A goldfinch nest when first constructed is among the most charming built by birds: solidly constructed of soft thistle and willow down, and other delicate plant fibers, it is felted together into a warm, watertight cup that is truly beautiful. Yet many goldfinches permit such very untidy conditions to develop that the nest is ringed by unsightly excrement by the time the young birds leave it. No estimate has been made of young goldfinch losses due to this slovenly housekeeping. For a brief time after the young have hatched, cliff swallows carry away the fecal sacs, but as they grow this task is neglected. The young birds back to the opening

Gannets (*Morus bassanus*)

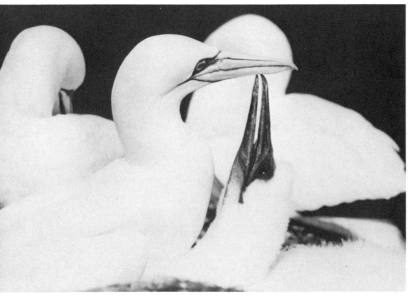

of the mud nest to defecate, keeping the nest clean, but in no time the wall of the barn or garage below is effectively "whitewashed." Almost from the first day of their lives, eagles, ospreys, and other raptors back to the edge of the nest and defecate over the rim. Kittiwakes, generally regarded in this country as birds of wild oceans and oceanic islands, nest on windowsills of buildings along the main street of Alesund, Norway. Many of these buildings have had to be vacated because of the unsanitary conditions after the young gulls hatch. Kittiwakes treated those buildings exactly as if they were sheer, oceanic cliffs, once the sole nesting place of these small gulls.

Anybody who has sailed by a large seabird colony or heron rookery has noted the whitewashing on rocks, trees, or shrubs. No attempt is made to conceal the colony, for there are always watchful eyes to discover predators and, if danger is sighted, the entire colony is quickly in an uproar. In a very dry climate, as on certain islands off the coast of Peru, excrement from seabirds, particularly that of guanay cormorants, accumulates. It is one of the best fertilizers in the world and is mined by the government. In fact, guano from the seabird colonies is one of the most valuable resources of Peru.

As we examine the clean nest of a chipping sparrow, made chiefly of horsehair wherever it is available, it is difficult to think of the lice, flies, and various insect larvae that may invade it and sometimes kill the young birds. The majority of young birds that nest in holes are probably infested with bird lice. Various types of larvae bite young birds so often they die. Ants, too, may invade a nest and kill them. Though the parents are most attentive to their young, there are many nest hazards they are unable to handle. Insect pests and parasites are two of these.

Some species of birds apparently enjoy a nursemaid system. It is not unusual to see three chimney swifts flying in unison as they sweep the air for insects, and later find that three birds, not just the usual two, are caring for the young swifts. In quite a different category of helpfulness is the bird that, hurrying to feed its young but distracted by the food cries of another species, stops to feed them. I know of one pair of dark-eyed juncos on an island in Maine that stopped many times to feed young song sparrows that were begging for food. It must be added, however, that song sparrows and juncos are rather closely related and food cries of the young are similar. Kingbirds and phoebes, which are both flycatchers, also interact in this way. In fact, kingbirds have been known to drive away the phoebes and take over the care of the young birds.

The Young Birds Fledge

As summer advances northward toward the Arctic, billions of helpless altricial birds are completely dependent on their parents for food, shelter, and protection. Among these are the blue jays, a widespread species both beautiful and intelligent. Though jays are noisy and sometimes downright raucous in public, in private life their voices are sometimes soft and occasionally even musical. The sexes look alike and both parents devote themselves to the care of their young. Until recently British ornithologists placed the *Corvidae* family, which includes crows, ravens, magpies, and jays, at the very top of the evolutionary scale of avian development, and many people who know these birds well think they belong in that lofty position. Their intelligence and ability to cope with varied situations are evident in many things they do.

In their nesting development jays are fairly typical of all young passerine birds. About three hours after a jay breaks out of the egg, it is able to lift its big head and wave it about frantically, presenting an enormous yellow-edged mouth to its parents as it implores them to pack it full of soft insects and larvae. In those few brief hours it has become an eating machine. Its greedy ingestion of great quantities of food enables it to grow with almost dizzying speed. The growth of a young jay, or any other altricial bird, is faster than that of other vertebrate animals.

For the first few days the young blue jay responds to a mere touch on the rim of the nest by opening its brightly colored mouth. At this tender age the blue jay and its nest mates cannot distinguish between their parents and an intruder; it may be that the sudden flash of color as those gaudy mouths spring open will startle some predators enough to frighten them away. By the time a blue jay is five days old, its eyes are open and fear behavior develops. Its mouth no longer springs open when an intruder approaches. Instead, it flattens itself in the nest and becomes motionless. Only when it sees or hears its parents does it lift its head and beg wildly for food.

At this time tightly sheathed feathers begin to sprout from tiny buds beneath the skin. The flight feathers grow most rapidly. The wings fold into a Z and open into a rigid plane that will eventually, when the flight feathers are fully grown, support flight. Feathers that shingle the body contours grow more slowly, while those on the neck and head develop last of all. When the blue jay is about nine days old, the sheaths begin to split from the feathers. During these days of rapid growth, the blue-jay nest becomes overcrowded as the three to six siblings strive for first place in the feeding line and move about seeking comfortable positions. There is much pushing and jostling as the birds stretch and yawn. They flap their small wings and peck themselves, the nest, and each other. They begin to groom their expanding feathers. By the time the jay is seventeen or eighteen days old, its natal down has been replaced with a feather pattern like that of its parents in shades of blue, black, and white. Except for its short tail and wing feathers, and large, fleshy yellow bill flanges, the young jay resembles an adult bird.

Between seventeen and twenty-one days, the young blue jay, which still has wisps of natal down sticking above the feathers on its head, is ready to fledge. Like children about to make their first dive into the cold water of spring, the jays crane their necks as they lean forward out of the nest and then draw back. Finally, one jay gains enough courage to spring from the nest, or perhaps it is pushed over the edge by its restless siblings. In a matter of minutes the nest is empty, as the other fledglings follow the leader. The first flight is brief and unsteady. Some land on a bush, some on the ground, but none returns to the nest. The parents lead the youngsters away and continue to feed them for several days. As the hungry fledglings follow their parents, their skill in flying grows rapidly and they begin to feed themselves.

Proper development of the flight feathers is essential for this important stage in a bird's life. Ostriches, penguins, and other species that cannot fly never fledge; though feathers may grow on their wings, neither those feathers nor the pectoral muscles that power the wings are adequate for flight.

In all the world, birds are the only animals that grow feathers, which are fantastically complicated structures. The shaft, sometimes called the quill, is the central rib or stem. The upper part of the shaft, with a row of barbs on either side, is called the rachis. The lower part of the shaft, which has no barbs, is named the calamus. Each barb has two rows of barbules; from these spring hooks called barbicels, which work like the teeth of a zipper into opposite grooves. They hook together so tightly that air cannot force its way through the feather. There are some nine hundred thousand to a million barbules on a single primary feather.

A feather is one of the lightest yet strongest materials grown by any creature. It is durable and flexible, a superb functional structure for flight. It is equally effective as an insulator. By the time a young bird fledges, its body feathers insulate it from both cold and heat.

The number of feathers covering each bird is enormous. During the summer, a ruby-throated hummingbird weighing no more than a penny has more than fifteen hundred feathers, a robin almost three thousand, while a whistling swan is clothed in more than twenty-five thousand. Birds that spend the winter in cold areas have thicker plumage during that season than they do the rest of the year.

Odd as it may seem, a feather does not begin its service for flight until it is dead. As it reaches the full size, the shaft is sealed off so the blood can no longer enter and feed it. It becomes lifeless, as our fingernails and hair do beyond a certain point. Nevertheless, if a feather is pulled out, a new one immediately begins growing to replace it. Feathers are produced by the skin, and are the most complex skin growth of any animal. Flight feathers are extremely elastic and as air pressures vary, they flex to meet each situation. They are very strong, yet very light. A male mute swan may tip the scale at thirty pounds, yet it would require a very sensitive instrument to weigh accurately his largest primary feather. Dropped from a height, it would float for some time on the most delicate breeze.

Our young blue jay in less than three weeks has clothed itself with a set of complicated feathers having extraordinary qualities. After its first short flight, it may end up on the ground, from which it will take off with great difficulty. Ravenous after the effort of launching itself into the air for the first time, it will hop after its parents. They may coax it to make further efforts by holding delicious larvae just beyond its reach so that in its eagerness it will fly a few more feet. Soon it is able to fly several yards, gaining skill and strength with each flight. First landings are invariably clumsy. As the ability to fly develops, so does landing competence, although the knack of making perfect landings is acquired much more slowly than the technique of flight itself.

A young jay is capable of complete independence by the time it is a month old, but it usually remains in a family group for a longer time learning what to eat and how to collect it. In his *Life Histories of North American Birds,* A. C. Bent notes that family ties may hold well into the first winter. During the experiment he cites, mice were trapped and placed on a feeding tray. Some of the jays, presumably the young of the previous summer, were afraid, but the knowledgeable older birds tore the mice to pieces. At this point the young birds came close and were fed bits of the mice by the adult jays. If this behavior of the jays was correctly interpreted, it means that some young jays have a much longer family life than is general among passerine species.

Pileated Woodpeckers (*Dryocopus pileatus*)

The anhinga is an ancient species that also exhibits a long development. Anhinga eggs hatch after an incubation of twenty-five to twenty-eight days. The altricial young are naked and helpless, but fed by both parents, they grow rapidly and are soon covered with dense, buff-colored down. By the time they are two weeks old they will jump off the nest into the water below when frightened. Then, when their fear subsides, they climb back, using their wings and neck as well as their toes. Many anhingas experience such a premature departure from their nest when two weeks old or older. The age when they fledge is not known. Their parents do not look alike, the male having a black breast, while that of the female is a pale, rich buff. When the fledglings leave the nest they resemble the female and will not achieve their adult plumage until mature at about two years.

Except for a brief period at the height of the courtship season, when the face and legs of the male white ibis are more intensely red than those of the female, both sexes look too much alike for us to tell which is which. Among passerine birds where the sexes look alike, as blue jays do, the fledglings look like their parents, but this is far from true with the look-alike white ibis. The offspring so little resemble their parents that for centuries they were regarded as a distinct species. The painter Mark Catesby called them Spanish curlews, as did the great naturalist William Bartram. Not until the time of John James Audubon, in the mid-1830s, were the so-called "Spanish curlews" recognized as immature white ibises. While young white ibises are growing they spend a lot of time climbing among the branches of bushes holding their nests. They fledge in about seven weeks, clothed in mottled dark brown and white plumage, with far less bare skin on their faces than on those of their parents.

Young roseate spoonbills look very pink when they are hatched because their rosy skin glows brightly through their first sparse white down. Like young white ibises, the young spoonbill climbs about in the bushes close to the nest before it fledges. Though its flight feathers are not fully grown, it leaves the nest for good when five or six weeks old. Like the young white ibis, it does not copy the appearance of its look-alike

Whooping Crane (*Grus americana*)

parents. Its spoon-shaped bill is pale and quite small and its head, unlike the naked head of the adult, is covered with down or feathers all the way to the bill. When its first, or juvenile, plumage is attained, it is white except for the palest tint of pink on the wings, while the tips of its primaries are dusky. The fledgling spoonbills gather in flocks along the shore of the nesting island when they are about six weeks old. There they practice flying and at the same time learn to feed themselves. When an adult appears it is mobbed by the fledglings, all bowing low, jerking their heads, and begging with high-pitched, whining cries. More often than not, their begging is fruitless, though occasionally one of the adults succumbs to the insistent pleas and opens its bill, permitting the fledgling to reach in for a feast. Judging from the few times that this happens, however, the young must learn quickly to feed themselves or they will starve. Few fledgling spoonbills really fly well before they are two months old.

Frederick Kent Truslow had the great good fortune, as well as a profound determination, to follow the day-by-day development of young bald eagles from the moment they hatched until they fledged, months later. As a result, we know the young are fed only three or four times a day. At first, the female stayed with the young eagles, taking the fish brought by its mate, tearing it to pieces, and feeding the eaglets. By the time they were three weeks old, the eaglets were left alone while both parents hunted for food.

There was ample room in the nest for the young birds to exercise freely. Sometimes they even appeared to play, tossing a twig in the air and pouncing on it as it fell. When the eaglets were six weeks old, their flight feathers were well developed, but the broad wings were still too weak to lift without a struggle. At nine weeks they began to leap a full three feet above the nest and as the days passed they managed to hover as much as ten feet over it. At twelve weeks, the parents stopped feeding the eaglets, but perched not far away, holding fish in their talons. Finally, the hungry young eagles were so starved that they simply had to fly, and fly they did, landing by their parents, who rewarded them with the fish. For some time the young eagles stayed with their parents in the vicinity of the nest, returning to it from time to time to use it as a dining table. The fledgling eagles were brown all over and would not develop the handsome white head and tail of an adult bird for at least three years, and perhaps even five years.

Ospreys, often called fish hawks, occur on every continent of the world except icy Antarctica. They are the only bird of prey whose sole food is fish. To catch its prey, the osprey dives feet first with great skill, only occasionally missing its target or striking a fish so large that the bird can be pulled beneath the surface and drowned. It eats mostly trash fish, but even so, it is not common enough in most places to arouse the enmity of human sport fishermen. In the British Isles, however, gamekeepers once shot these birds, believing that they had no right to take fish that sportsmen like to kill. Of all hawk eggs, those of the osprey are the most beautiful, with spots and blotches of red, brown, and chocolate on a white background. The eggs used to be coveted by collectors so that, between the gamekeepers and egg collectors, the osprey was thought to have been wiped out as a nesting bird in Britain late in the nineteenth century. Then, in 1958, a nesting pair was discovered in Scotland. Immediately a round-the-clock watch was set up to protect the rare nest and its inhabitants. The young birds fledged successfully. Now several nests are known there and, guarded from attack, the birds may succeed in an area where once they were routinely persecuted. In spite of vigilance, some eggs are still stolen by collectors.

An osprey nest looks like a large pile of plant materials. The bird may carry in its talons sticks up to five feet in length to it. The same nest is used for several years and grows in size annually as more sticks are

Golden Eagle (*Aquila chrysaetos*)

added to it. Usually the nest is built in a tree, but on Gardiners Island in Long Island Sound, which once supported the largest osprey colony in the world, as many as sixty nests were counted on the ground in one summer. Ospreys also nest on utility poles, crags, and ledges, and on wheels especially erected on poles for them. The handsome eggs are incubated from twenty-eight days to five weeks, and the young birds remain in the nest from eight to ten weeks before they fledge. As feathers clothe the young ospreys, they look much like their parents, although they have less white on the head and their plumage is more mottled. Their eyes are orange-yellow and will not take on the pale yellow of the adult until they are old enough to breed. Like many hawks, ospreys return to their nests after fledging and use them to dine on.

Pileated woodpeckers incubate their eggs about eighteen days, a duty shared by both parents, with the male usually taking the night shift. The young are born completely naked, but unlike most birds, they do not pass through a stage when they are covered with down; they develop their first, or juvenile, plumage right

away and are ready to fledge at twenty-three to twenty-five days after hatching. Having matured sufficiently to launch themselves from the nesting cavity, they fly away strongly with the typical undulating woodpecker flight.

Tree swallows are common nesting birds that occupy small, natural cavities, woodpecker holes, and bird boxes provided by people. Except for the band of southern states, they are breeding birds across most of the United States and almost as far as trees grow to normal size before their northward march is halted by sub-Arctic cold. In smooth brown juvenile plumage, young tree swallows crowd to the entrance of their cavity nest a day or two before they fledge, two of them often pushing their heads out at once and giving the impression that they may fall at any moment. As is true of most other hole-nesting birds (young wood ducks are among the exceptions), tree swallows are slow to fledge and stay in the nest between twenty and twenty-four days. Once they leap into the air, however, they fly skillfully. For a few days after fledging, the young birds often perch on a twig or wire

Ospreys (*Pandion haliaetus*)

to rest, receiving occasional food from their parents.

Close to and within the Arctic Circle, where on early summer days the sun does not set at all, parent birds bring their young to the fledging stage more quickly than in the shorter days of the temperate zone. One Arctic warbler in Alaska was discovered feeding its young on an eighteen-hour daily schedule. Comparative studies have been made of the feeding schedules of Ohio robins and those in northern Alaska. The former fed their hatchlings over a period of sixteen hours, making ninety-six feedings in an average day until the young fledged at thirteen days. The Alaska robins, enjoying longer hours of daylight, took food to their young for twenty-one hours, averaging one hundred and thirty-seven daily feedings. The latter youngsters matured much faster and fledged when they were only nine days old. Rapid development to the fledging stage naturally increases the chances of the young birds to survive, for open nests are extremely vulnerable. It appears that the amount of food the young receive influences the time it takes for them to fledge, and that amount is affected by both the availability of food and the number of daylight hours.

As birds grow, they move about more vigorously in the nest and spend much time exercising—flapping their wings and sometimes leaping into the air above the nest. These flying exercises may be beneficial, but it has been proved conclusively that it is age rather than exercise that determines the fledging time. Collars were placed on pigeons so they could not move their wings at all, and when these were removed at fledging time the young birds flew as skillfully as their unrestrained relatives of the same age.

Altricial birds are cared for in the nest by their parents until their flight feathers are well grown, but some precocial birds have a problem, for they leave the nest long before they have any feathers at all, let alone the ability to fly. Those that nest on the ground, of course, only have to walk away from it, but some precocial birds, including several species of ducks, nest in trees. When young wood ducks, for instance, are dry and fluffy, the mother coaxes them to leave the nest, which may be in a cavity an awesome fifty feet above the ground. But the youngsters are ready for this adventure; they climb up the wall of the cavity, even if it is almost perpendicular, using their sharp, pinpointed claws and the hooked nails on the tips of their bills. The birds are light as thistledown at this stage and

flutter down from the great height, waving their tiny wings and spreading their webbed toes, which may slow their tumble somewhat. After they land safely, they are led to the nearest water by their attentive mother.

The only precocial upland game bird in North America that builds its nest in a tree is the chachalaca of south Texas, a bird that hatches with partly grown primary feathers. It belongs to the order Galliformes as do the extraordinary megapodes, which fledge more quickly than any other species in the world and actually fly soon after they leave the egg. Young chachalacas do not fledge that quickly, but one of them, hatched by a domestic hen, has managed to fly a short distance when only a day old. It is easy to see that they would have no trouble dropping to the ground from a nest in a tree as soon as their down is dry.

Clearly there is no hard-and-fast rule for the age at which birds fledge, but regardless of the time it takes, fledging brings every bird into the most dangerous stage of life—its first year of independence.

Immature White Ibis (*Eudocimus albus*)

Dispersal

Summer days begin to shorten even as heat intensifies and insect hordes continue to multiply. As the hot, fruitful days advance, the reproductive segment of the annual cycle of birds moves inexorably to its conclusion. The ardent emotions of spring fade. No longer when a gannet returns to the nest does its partner respond by facing him eagerly as he invites her to bill with him. The plumes of the great egret grow tattered and are lifted halfheartedly, if at all, in greeting its mate. The Arctic tern fails to bring a silver fish to its consort. Cedar waxwings no longer present their mates with choice berries.

As the signals of affection lapse, the bonds holding the pairs together weaken and finally dissolve. Yet in a few species the bonds remain intact at the end of the nesting season, and for some they will last a lifetime. Pair bonds between certain swans, geese, and lovebirds are among the small number that endure. Some of these birds, having lost a mate, never take another. But with most species the pair bond lasts only for one swing of the breeding cycle. When two or more broods are reared in a single season, more often than not partners are changed between broods. The bonds between parents and young begin to fray as the season progresses. You can almost hear the snapping of the links as mate ignores mate, and as adult birds abandon the young on whom they have lavished so much attention.

The fiery red of the male scarlet tanager fades and its back becomes green and its underparts yellow. Male bobolinks, indigo buntings, and rose-breasted grosbeaks lose their handsome springtime dress and become nearly as drab as the females. Many species of warblers lose their distinctive spring patterns and colors, becoming, as Roger Tory Peterson says, "confusing fall warblers," because birders then find great difficulty in identifying them.

Even though their plumage may not change radically in looks when care of the young ends, often the adults have worn, shabby feathers. These are renewed by a molt among some species before migration begins. Canada geese lose so many feathers at one time that for a brief period they are unable to fly, and they seek the security of large bodies of water while their new feathers grow. Songbirds become secretive, and even ardent birders find field observations unrewarding at this time.

The young birds have changed in appearance, too. Once their baby down is replaced by feathers, the will of their parents to feed them seems to evaporate among gannets, cormorants, pelicans, and many other species. The bright mouth colors of young passerine birds fade, and the adults are no longer feverishly stimulated to stuff them with caterpillars and insects. After the young fledge, parental feeding becomes desultory and soon stops altogether.

Young grebes may experience a more painful parting with their parents than other young birds. To begin with, as infants they are given unusually tender care, for soon after they break out of the egg incubated by both sexes, each baby grebe climbs aboard the back of one of its parents and snuggles deep in the soft, warm feathers.

For several days the young grebes spend most of their time protected on their parents' backs, and only a puffy look about those back feathers gives a clue that a young grebe is riding there. As they grow, they begin to take an interest in the world around them, increasingly lifting their heads above the feathers to survey their surroundings. When the adult grebe dives for a fish, the young bird may stay aboard. When the speed of the submarine chase is great, the young passenger may be dislodged and pop to the surface like a cork. Young grebes do not dive well until they are several weeks old, a skill at which they must become adept before they can feed themselves. But they spend much time swimming and occasionally are refused a ride even though they beg with high-pitched, whining cries.

For well over two months the parents feed their steadily growing young. More than 75 percent of their food is made up of small fish, which the grebes pursue under water and spear with their rapier-sharp bills. The adults never teach their offspring, but the young grebes, like all young birds, are great imitators and no doubt learn much by watching their parents. Finally, after months of devotion to eggs and young, the day comes when the parents have had it. They incubated their eggs for more than three weeks, then patiently carried their young on their backs, protected them, and fed them day after day. The time has come to wean them. The young birds seem chagrined and dismayed by the sudden change in their parents and persist in following them about, whining for food. Exasperated at last, the parents turn on the young grebes and fiercely drive them away, wielding those sharp bills used so expertly in spearing fish. There are records of western grebes becoming so furious with their clinging young that they killed them. Usually, however, after making their rejection of the young grebes very plain, the adults move to a different part of the area.

All through the bird world the age and manner in which the young finally become independent vary, as does their behavior when at last they are on their own. Even among species as closely related as white and brown pelicans the difference is dramatic.

White pelicans, with a wingspread of about nine feet, nest on the ground. By the time the young are three or four weeks old they are very fat and covered with dense, light gray down. They waddle away from the nest with still useless wings held limply outstretched, and gather in large pods. If frightened, they will leave the island, swimming away in a compact crowd, often shepherded by a few adults. When an adult comes to the island, the young birds mob it in a wild scramble, all begging for food. But the parents appear to know their own offspring and they will feed only theirs, rewarding the other insistent birds with a sharp peck. The young birds, having been good swimmers from the moment they trudged from the nest, are able to feed themselves before they make their first flight at about two months. Most of these pelicans grow up within the frost belt and must move south to open water to spend the winter.

All brown pelicans nest in the warmer sections of our country, always near salt or brackish water, and sometimes on the ground. In Florida most nest in bushes, particularly in mangroves, where water may wash under them. Mortality among the young is very high. Very small pelicans may be eaten by larger ones, and occasionally a parent will pick up an infant and throw it out of the nest. At a fairly early age the pelicans begin to clamber about in the bushes, but this frequently ends in disaster. Some hang themselves, some are trapped in the crotch of branches, and some simply land on the ground or in the water, where they starve to death.

Brown pelicans make their first flight when about nine weeks old, but their parents continue to feed them for some time afterward. The young pelican not only must become skilled in flight so it can journey to a suitable area to dive for its food, it must be able to pinpoint its prey from a height, make an accurate plunge, and catch the fish in its bill, a technique that requires considerable practice before it is perfected.

Gannets and boobies on their oceanic island cliffs are deserted by their parents once they are well fledged, and they stay on the nest until they have lost much of their baby fat. On their first flight, at about thirteen weeks, they usually glide to a splash-down in the ocean from which they may be unable to rise for a week or more. Finally, having lost their excess weight, they make it into the air, and instinct tells them how to fish. It is not long before they begin wandering to far-off places in search of food.

Many young birds are able to feed on readily available food materials even if their heritage compels them to dive for their food or to obtain it in some other way. But some birds are so specialized that they may starve in the midst of plenty if they cannot get their food in the traditional way. Black skimmers, because of their strange bills, probably could not pick up food on land even if they tried. Their bills are designed specifically for skimming close to the water, touching a small fish with the under mandible, then closing the upper mandible on it as the prey is forced upward by water pressure. Before it can fish for itself, the young skimmer must become very adept at flight, and while its method of skimming is instinctive, it is likely that the young bird learns by imitating the parents. The time when it becomes independent is not known, but in early autumn mixed flocks of skimmers made up of black-backed adults and dark-brown-backed juveniles may be observed on mud flats and sandbars.

Herons, ibises, and spoonbills all take rather similar paths to independence. They are fed by their parents after fledging until they fly fairly well. They usually do not disperse very widely but may travel a few hundred miles from their nesting area. Most swans, ducks, and geese, however, nest where winter is severe and the waters freeze over. Therefore, they are forced to find open water where they can rest and feed during the winter months. Swans and geese generally stay in family groups until the following spring unless they are broken up by hunters or natural disasters.

Some young ducks may be weaned at the tender age of three weeks. They cannot fly at that age, but they are able to feed themselves. Ducks are very gregarious, and when migration time arrives the flight of the young ducks is strong and direct. If they join a flock of adults, they are capable of maintaining adequate speed. Even those that migrate without adult guidance find the ancestral wintering place without difficulty.

The northern tundra is the favored nesting place for many shorebirds. Before they can fly the young are abandoned by their parents, who immediately begin a southward migration that may take them to the most southern lands of the earth. The young must feed themselves and learn to use their wings by instinctive programming. Well before the first severe weather of autumn, most of the young shorebirds set off, having gathered into flocks of their own kind, each maintaining the same distance from its neighbor even while changing position, moving as if they were a single unit. The speed of these small birds as they dart forward without a leader, each executing its part in the most intricate movements, is one of the most inexplicable sights in nature. They fly southward without any guidance on a journey of thousands of miles and invariably arrive at the place where their ancestors traditionally wintered.

Almost all fledgling gulls have rather dull brown or gray mottled plumage completely unlike that of their snowy-bodied parents. Nevertheless, by the time they become independent, their powers of flight are well developed. Youth is an adventurous time of life among humans, and the same is true of young gulls. They often travel farther in their first few months of independence than they ever will again. Young herring gulls banded in Maine have been reported as far south as Panama, far beyond the normal wintering range of the species.

As we have already seen, Arctic terns are among the greatest travelers in the world, and it is not surprising that their young make spectacular journeys soon after they become independent. One young Arctic tern banded in Labrador by Dr. Oliver Austin was picked up on the coast of France less than six weeks later. Another reached the coast of Natal in about ninety days, some nine thousand miles from its nesting place. Still another, banded on the west coast of Greenland, was picked up on the coast of Africa, more than ten thousand miles from its birthplace.

Not all young birds follow the routes traveled by their parents. Adult golden plovers that nest in the Arctic go south as far as Patagonia, crossing the Atlantic by way of Bermuda. Their young end up in the same wintering area, but they fly south across Canada, down the Mississippi River Valley to Central America and then to Argentina. The behavior of juvenile lapwings in England is even more puzzling. They migrate before the adults and, without any guidance, find

Trumpeter Swans (*Olor buccinator*)

their way to Africa, the winter home of their species.

Many hawks, eagles, and owls stay in the nest a long time. Size seems to influence the nest period of raptors, for some of the small falcons leave the nest in about a month, while a bald eagle remains there for twelve weeks. Both turkey and black vultures make their first flights when eight to ten weeks old, but the California condor waits four months or more before taking off for its first flight.

Small passerine birds fledge in about two weeks, and hop about more than they fly for a few days while their parents continue to feed and brood them. But then the birds disperse, each in the way of its own species. Sparrows gather in flocks to feed. Swifts, which stay in the nest as long as six weeks, may immediately begin their migration at the time of their first flight. Ravens tend to stay in sibling groups, spreading out to feed, but keeping in touch by calling and periodically gathering to perch together in trees.

Some young birds begin their juvenile life by taking up a solitary existence, as ruffed grouse do, while others, like swans, geese, and cranes, become junior members of the adult society. Shorebirds join other juniors, usually of their own kind. Swallows, sparrows, buntings, and blackbirds simply join mixed flocks that may be segregated as to species and sex, or may be a mixture of many species and both sexes.

When the time comes to fend for themselves, most young birds find an abundance of the kind of food they need so they are able to build up their flight strength for whatever migration lies ahead. Confidence in their ability to fly, to find food, and to cope with their life situation grows quickly as their flight feathers lengthen and their weight becomes normal for their species.

These early days of juvenile independence are fraught with danger. Guided by instinct though they are, the young birds are ignorant, often careless, and unaware of many perils in their environment. Weather, disease, and accidents take their toll, and often it is a heavy one. The greatest loss, however, is from predation. Sharp-shinned hawks must catch food for their young and so they often wreak havoc among newflown swallows that have not yet acquired the power and skill that maturity will give them. But there is scarcely an animal in the world that is not a predator on other animal life during at least part of its life. Even the exquisite nectar-eating hummingbird adds tiny insects and spider eggs to its diet. Without predation by the birds, mammals, and reptiles that eat eggs and young birds, we would soon be inundated by them. Robins often have two broods of four each during a season. Should all these survive and enjoy a similar breeding rate, the original pair would have 19,500,000 descendants in only ten years. Those of us living in the southern United States who have holly, pyracantha, and other trees producing small fruits beloved by robins know that even two hundred robins at one time are too many as we temporarily surrender our patios to their flocks. Always enough robins manage to survive the dangers they meet, though so many of them become food for other creatures. When the next nesting season arrives, the surplus will have been cropped, and approximately the same number of robins will occupy territories as did the preceding year. One researcher found that of five hundred and forty-eight robin eggs, 57.8 percent hatched and 44.9 percent fledged. We do not know how many of these robins that fledged escaped the dangers of the juvenile period and survived to return to their nesting regions the following spring, but it is estimated that 95 percent of all the hatchlings each year do not live to see their first birthday.

In 1850 Henry David Thoreau wrote, "Now about the first of September, you will see flocks of small birds forming compact and distinct masses, as if they were not only animated by one spirit but actually held together by some invisible fluid or film, and will hear the sound of their wings rippling or fanning the air as they flow through it. . . . Their mind must operate faster than man's, in proportion as their bodies do."

It is said that birds sacrificed the chance to forge ahead intellectually because of their wonderful powers of flight, for they can escape danger by sudden withdrawal instead of by guile. They can move from a place poor in food to one that is rich in a matter of hours; they can even abandon the cold and be warm if they wish. And so they live only in the present at a high pitch of emotional excitement. Their complex instincts, their amazing skills, their beautiful colors and patterns, and their music stir our imagination, but of all their attributes, the ability to fly is the most exciting.

Once the birds reach their wintering places, their annual cycle settles to its lowest, most inactive point. The adults renew their energies after a season of hectic, unremitting activity. The new generation they reared is on its own, facing incalculable dangers, but nature, looking forward, already is molding the young birds so they will be prepared for the time when they, in turn, assume the burden of raising another generation. As those birds made their first migratory flight, they had no awareness, no conception of what the future held for them.

They had joined the river of life, a river that had changed immeasurably since the dawn of time. Their ancestors had joined it some one hundred and eighty million years ago, long before the first man. Annually the river of life sweeps the newest generation forward in the inexorable movement of time. Obeying incomprehensible impulses, they follow the ancient traditions of their kind as if they knew the reasons behind their behavior and the purpose of it all.

Index of Latin Names

A

American Avocet   *Recurvirostra americana*
American Golden Plover   *Pluvialis dominica*
American Kestrel   *Falco sparverius*
American Redstart   *Setophaga ruticilla*
American Robin   *Turdus migratorius*
American White Pelican   *Pelecanus erythrorhynchos*
American Woodcock   *Philohela minor*
Anhinga   *Anhinga anhinga*
Arctic Tern   *Sterna paradisaea*
Arctic Warbler   *Phylloscopus borealis*

B

Bald Eagle   *Haliaeetus leucocephalus*
Baltimore (Northern) Oriole   *Icterus galbula*
Barn Owl   *Tyto alba*
Barn Swallow   *Hirundo rustica*
Barnacle Goose   *Branta leucopsis*
Barred Owl   *Strix varia*
Bar-tailed Godwit   *Limosa lapponica*
Bay-breasted Warbler   *Dendroica castanea*
Bearded Tit   *Panurus biarmicus*
Bee Hummingbird   *Mellisuga helenae*
Black-bellied Plover   *Pluvialis squatarola*
Black-billed Magpie   *Pica pica*
Black-capped Chickadee   *Parus atricapillus*
Black-headed Gull   *Larus ridibundus*
Black-legged Kittiwake   *Rissa tridactyla*
Black-necked Stilt   *Himantopus mexicanus*
Black Skimmer   *Rynchops niger*
Black Tern   *Chlidonias niger*
Black Vulture   *Coragyps atratus*
Blue-footed Booby   *Sula nebouxii*
Blue Jay   *Cyanocitta cristata*
Boat-tailed Grackle   *Cassidix major*
Bobolink   *Dolichonyx oryzivorus*
Bobwhite   *Colinus virginianus*
Brewer's Sparrow   *Spizella breweri*
Brown-headed Cowbird   *Molothrus ater*
Brown-headed Nuthatch   *Sitta pusilla*
Brown Kiwi   *Apteryx australis*
Brown Pelican   *Pelecanus occidentalis*
Brown Thrasher   *Toxostema rufum*
Burrowing Owl   *Spectyto cunicularia*
Bushtit   *Psaltriparus minimus*

C

California Condor   *Gymnogyps californianus*
California Gull   *Lurus californicus*
Canada Goose   *Branta canadensis*
Canada Warbler   *Wilsonia canadensis*
Canvasback   *Aythya valisineria*
Canyon Wren   *Catherpes mexicanus*
Cardinal   *Cardinalis cardinalis*
Carolina Wren   *Thryothorus ludovicianus*
Cave Swallow   *Petrochelidon fulva*
Cedar Waxwing   *Bombycilla cedrorum*
Chachalaca   *Ortalis vetula*
Chestnut-sided Warbler   *Dendroica pensylvanica*
Chimney Swift   *Chaetura pelagica*
Chipping Sparrow   *Spizella passerina*
Chuck-will's-widow   *Caprimulgus carolinensis*
Clark's Nutcracker   *Nucifraga columbiana*
Cliff Swallow   *Petrochelidon pyrrhonota*
Common Cuckoo   *Cuculus canorus*
Common Crane   *Grus grus*
Common Eider   *Somateria mollissima*
Common Gallinule   *Gallinula chloropus*
Common Murre (Guillemot in Europe)   *Uria aalge*
Common Puffin   *Fratercula arctica*
Common Raven   *Corvus corax*
Common Tern   *Sterna hirundo*
Crested Oropendola   *Psarocolius decumanus*

D

Dark-eyed Junco   *Junco hyemalis*
Double-crested Cormorant   *Phalacrocorax auritus*

E

Eastern Kingbird   *Tyrannus tyrannus*
Egyptian Plover   *Pluvianus aegyptius*
Egyptian Vulture   *Neophron percnopterus*
Elegant Tern   *Sterna elegans*
Emperor Penguin   *Aptenodytes forsteri*
Emu   *Dromaius novaehollandiae*
Everglade Kite   *Rostrhamus sociabilis*

F

Fairy Tern   *Gygis alba*
Field Sparrow   *Spizella pusilla*
Fox Sparrow   *Passerella iliaca*
Franklin's Gull   *Larus pipixcan*

G

Gadwall   *Anas strepera*
Gannet   *Morus bassanus*
Golden-crowned Kinglet   *Regulus satrapa*
Golden Eagle   *Aquila chrysaetos*
Goliath Heron   *Ardea goliath*
Gray Catbird   *Dumetella carolinensis*
Gray-crowned Rosy Finch   *Leucosticte tephrocotis*
Gray Jay   *Perisoreus canadensis*
Great Black-backed Gull   *Larus marinus*
Great Blue Heron   *Ardea herodias*
Great Crested Flycatcher   *Myiarchus crinitus*
Great Elephant Bird   *Aepyornis maximus*
Great Egret   *Casmerodius albus*
Great Horned Owl   *Bubo virginianus*
Great Tinamou   *Tinamous major*
Greater Prairie Chicken   *Tympanuchus cupido*
Guanay Cormorant   *Phalacrocorax bougainvillii*

H

Hermit Thrush   *Catharus guttatus*
Herring Gull   *Larus argentatus*
Horned Lark   *Eremophila alpestris*
House Sparrow   *Passer domesticus*
House Wren   *Troglodytes aedon*

I

Indigo Bunting   *Passerina cyanea*
Ivory-billed Woodpecker   *Campephilus principalis*
Ivory Gull   *Pagophila eburnea*

J

Jungle Peafowl   *Pavo cristatus*

K

Killdeer   *Charadrius vociferus*
Kirtland's Warbler   *Dendroica kirtlandii*

L

Lapland Longspur   *Calcarius lapponicus*
Lapwing   *Vanellus vanellus*
Lark Bunting   *Calamospiza melanocorys*
Leach's Storm-petrel   *Oceanodroma leucorhoa*
Least Bittern   *Ixobrychus exilis*
Least Tern   *Sterna albifrons*
Lewis' Woodpecker   *Asyndesmus lewis*
Lichtenstein's Oriole   *Icterus gularis*
Limpkin   *Aramus guarauna*
Little Bittern   *Ixobrychus minutus*
Long-billed Curlew   *Numenius americanus*
Long-billed Marsh Wren   *Cistothorus palustris*
Long-tailed Tailorbird   *Orthotomus sutorius*

M

Magnificent Frigate   *Fregata magnificens*
Mallee Fowl   *Leipoa ocellata*
Marbled Godwit   *Limosa fedoa*
Mockingbird   *Mimus polyglottos*
Mountain Bluebird   *Sialia currucoides*
Mourning Dove   *Zenaida macroura*
Mute Swan   *Cygnus olor*

N

Nightingale   *Erithacus megarhynchos*
Noddy Tern   *Anous stolidus*
Northern Parula Warbler   *Parula americana*

O

Oilbird   *Steatornis caripensis*
Oldsquaw   *Clangula hyemalis*
Osprey   *Pandion haliaetus*
Ostrich   *Struthio camelus*

P

Painted Redstart   *Setophaga picta*
Palm Swift   *Cypsiurus parvus*
Peregrine Falcon   *Falco peregrinus*
Phainopepla   *Phainopepla nitens*
Pied-billed Grebe   *Podilymbus podiceps*
Pileated Woodpecker   *Dryocopus pileatus*
Poor-will   *Phalaenoptilus nuttallii*
Prothonotary Warbler   *Protonotaria citrea*

R

Red-bellied Woodpecker   *Centurus carolinus*
Reddish Egret   *Dichromanassa rufescens*
Redhead   *Aythya americana*
Redstart   *Phoenicurus phoenicurus*
Red-tailed Hawk   *Buteo jamaicensis*
Red-winged Blackbird   *Agelaius phoeniceus*
Ring-necked Pheasant   *Phasianus colchicus*
Robin   *Erithacus rubecula*
Rock Dove   *Columba livia*
Roseate Spoonbill   *Ajaia ajaja*
Roseate Tern   *Sterna dougallii*
Rose-breasted Grosbeak   *Pheucticus ludovicianus*
Rough-legged Hawk   *Buteo lagopus*
Royal Tern   *Sterna maxima*
Ruby-throated Hummingbird   *Archilochus colubris*
Ruddy Duck   *Oxyura jamaicensis*
Ruffed Grouse   *Bonasa umbellus*
Rufous Hornero   *Furnarius rufus*

S

Sandhill Crane   *Grus canadensis*
Scarlet Tanager   *Piranga olivacea*
Screech Owl   *Otus asio*
Seaside Sparrow   *Ammospiza maritima*
Sharp-shinned Hawk   *Accipiter striatus*
Skylark   *Alauda arvensis*
Smooth-billed Ani   *Crotophaga ani*
Snowy Egret   *Egretta thula*
Snowy Plover   *Charadrius alexandrinus*
Snowy Owl   *Nyctea scandiaca*
Song Sparrow   *Melospiza melodia*
Sooty Tern   *Sterna fuscata*
Spotted Sandpiper   *Actitis macularia*
Sprague's Pipit   *Anthus spragueii*
Spruce Grouse   *Canachites canadensis*
Starling   *Sturnis vulgaris*
Swallow-tailed Gull   *Creagrus furcatus*
Swallow-tailed Kite   *Elanoides forficatus*

T

Tree Swallow   *Iridoprocne bicolor*
Trumpeter Swan   *Olor buccinator*
Turkey   *Meleagris gallopavo*
Turkey Vulture   *Cathartes aura*

V

Verdin   *Auriparus flaviceps*
Vermilion Flycatcher   *Pyrocephalus rubinus*
Vervain Hummingbird   *Mellisuga minima*
Vesper Sparrow   *Pooecetes gramineus*

W

Wandering Albatross   *Diomedea exulans*
Water Pipit   *Anthus spinoletta*
Western Grebe   *Aechmophorus occidentalis*
Western Tanager   *Piranga ludoviciana*
Whip-poor-will   *Caprimulgus vociferus*
Whistling Swan   *Olor columbianus*
White Ibis   *Eudocimus albus*
White Stork   *Ciconia ciconia*
White-tailed Nightjar   *Caprimulgus cayennensis*
White-tailed Ptarmigan   *Lagopus leucurus*
White-throated Sparrow   *Zonotrichia albicollis*

White-throated Swift   *Aeronautes saxatalis*
Whooping Crane   *Grus americana*
Willow Ptarmigan   *Lagopus lagopus*
Wood Duck   *Aix sponsa*
Wood Stork   *Mycteria americana*
Wood Thrush   *Hylocichla mustelina*
Woodpecker Finch   *Camarhynchus pallidus*

Y

Yellow-headed Blackbird   *Xanthocephalus xanthocephalus*
Yellow-shafted (Common) Flicker   *Colaptes auratus*
Yellow Warbler   *Dendroica petechia*

The Bird Photographs of Frederick Kent Truslow

The Breeding Cycle Begins

Though the handsome plumes on the head of the great blue heron are few in number they are essential to a successful courtship. By displaying them the heron gives the signals needed to win a mate. To attract the opposite sex, the males of some species, such as the oriole, wear colorful nuptial plumage; the wood thrush sings beautiful songs, while others perform ritualized dances like the whooping crane's or complex aerial flights like the woodcock's.

Overleaf:
Courtship rituals vary with each species. Though the egrets, ibises, roseate spoonbills, and wood storks feeding in this pond have a superficial resemblance, there is no danger of interbreeding. If one species attempts to woo another, it will give the wrong signals or fail to give the correct one. The courting birds will immediately lose interest and seek a proper response to their signals elsewhere.

Below: The courtship ritual of the western grebe is as graceful as a ballet. This pair at the Bear River Migratory Bird Refuge, Utah, begins the first movement of a complex mutual display that will lead to the establishment of a pair bond.

These California gulls, amicably billing, are strengthening a bond already established after many pursuit flights, loud calls, bowing displays, and feeding of the female by the male.

Right: Common gallinules in Everglades National Park battle for dominance over a nesting territory. Once the nest is built, constant border fighting would disrupt the required peaceful home life of the birds, so the integrity of the territory must be established early. The establishment of the territory is usually the prerogative of the male.

Like many oceanic species, gannets nest in crowded colonies, each pair occupying an area of about two and a half feet square. If a gannet lands outside its own territory, turmoil erupts. Strong pointed beaks slash the intruder, who is here bloodied for its lack of judgment.

Fred Truslow took particular care not to disturb a nest. He struggled to maintain the delicate balance that would allow him to take the best possible photograph and at the same time not alarm the parent birds. In this photograph of nesting wood storks at Cuthbert Rookery, Florida, not one of the hundreds of birds is in the air. If his plane had flown just a bit lower the birds might have panicked and taken flight. These wood storks began nesting activities at the Cuthbert Rookery in January 1959, gathering by the hundreds until the low mangroves were covered by the big birds.

Once wood storks assume their adult plumage, they keep it as long as they live. Though there is no plumage change for the nesting season, the feet become brighter pink, the blackish bill may be lightly brushed here and there with red, and the naked, warty head becomes speckled with yellow.

Left: Two female common flickers battle over a good habitat and the male who dominates it.

Left, below: As the male makes chips fly with his vigorous digging, the strongest contender for his favors drives off the loser.

Right: The victorious female joins the male. After a mutual display they drop to the ground to mate. The male then surrenders the task of digging the nest hole to the female, who completes it.

Overleaf:
This pair of bald eagles returned annually to their nest atop a twenty-foot mangrove on Murray Key, Florida Bay, until it was destroyed by Hurricane Donna. Each year they renewed the pair bond with an aerial courtship and then added fresh sticks to the bulky nest.

The Eggs

The large eggs of a black skimmer are heavily
marked with dark spots and scrawls that render them
almost invisible in their shallow scrape nest on an
oceanic beach. The female alone incubates them.

Common puffins dig nest burrows on some oceanic
islands and may carry vegetable matter into them.
On Machias Seal Island, Maine, they lay their single
egg under a rock, usually without any nesting
material. This photograph shows an unusual nest in
which carefully crisscrossed plant stems indicate a
faint vestige of nest-making, though the egg is not
protected by them.

One calm, sleepy afternoon, April 16, 1966, waiting in a blind on a twelve-foot tower near a pileated woodpecker nest in Everglades National Park, Fred Truslow did not expect any action for some time, since an exchange of nest duties had just been made. But he did not relax his attention, and when the unexpected happened, he was ready to record it. Without warning, the top of the tree trunk crashed to the ground, the break uncovering the top of the woodpecker nest. The incubating female looked around, as dazed by the event as we would be should the roof of our home suddenly be lifted off.

Recovering, she backed down to her eggs and reappeared with an egg held crosswise in her mouth. This she juggled about until the large end was firmly wedged toward her throat. She flew off with it but soon returned.

The second egg and then the last were carried off in the same way in the same direction. Fred Truslow hoped they were deposited in one of the roosting cavities used by the pair, but no amount of searching verified this. These photographs form a unique record of a bird taking what appears to be responsible action when a disaster occurred. A new facet to our knowledge of bird behavior was added by the alert photographer. Pictures documenting this heretofore unproven aspect of bird behavior caused quite a stir among professional ornithologists, who might have discounted a verbal account of the behavior but could not question the truth of the photographs.

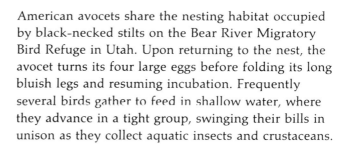

American avocets share the nesting habitat occupied by black-necked stilts on the Bear River Migratory Bird Refuge in Utah. Upon returning to the nest, the avocet turns its four large eggs before folding its long bluish legs and resuming incubation. Frequently several birds gather to feed in shallow water, where they advance in a tight group, swinging their bills in unison as they collect aquatic insects and crustaceans.

On the vast level reaches of the great Bear River Migratory Bird Refuge in Utah, Fred Truslow was the first ever to record in color the action of black-necked stilts faced with the loss of their four eggs when water threatened to inundate the nest. Truslow had placed his blind about eighteen feet from the nest and set to work, ignoring a west wind that gradually increased in violence until it threatened to topple the blind. Suddenly the stilts went into a veritable frenzy of action. Water from distant marshes, pushed before the fury of the wind, had crept across the dry earth until it looked like a lake. Water was rising around the nest and the stilts swiftly gathered mud and vegetable matter, using it to build up the nest one side at a time and rolling the eggs up to the higher levels. The birds added a full four and a half inches to the nest before they were satisfied that their eggs were safe. Finally, incubation was resumed.

The barred owl is a widespread species that usually nests in the cavity of a tree, but when you spend enough time observing wildlife you soon discover surprising exceptions to customary behavior. This owl was photographed on February 6, 1963, as she incubated her eggs on the ground near Seven-mile Tower in Everglades National Park. A barred-owl nest on the ground in an area of many trees had never before been recorded. This owl reared four sets of young here in as many years in spite of numerous meat-hungry neighbors—alligators, bobcats, opossums, and raccoons.

Everglade kites secure their nests to sinuous grasses and reeds growing far from shore in shallow areas of Lake Okeechobee in Florida. Gusty winds often tip the eggs of this endangered species into the water.

Eastern kingbirds are small but fierce and will attack
any bird, even an eagle, that flies near their nest.
They are equally intolerant of their own kind.
Though the sight of two females of any species
sharing the task of incubating eggs in the same nest
is virtually unknown, it is especially remarkable
when normally aggressive kingbirds do so, as in this
photograph.

Brilliantly colored prothonotary warblers are seldom
seen far from water. They place their moss-lined
nests in tree cavities or old hollowed stumps. Here
the female incubates her speckled pinkish eggs in a
swamp near Wadesboro, North Carolina.

Overleaf:
Because the American woodcock is active during the
dim light of dawn and twilight, it is not often seen,
though it is a rather common bird. Females alone
care for the eggs and chicks. This woodcock
incubating her four eggs in a slightly lined
depression on the ground blends with her
surroundings so completely that she is almost
invisible.

In contrast to the slight nest of a woodcock, an osprey builds a bulky one. Usually it is placed high in a tree, on a rock pinnacle, or on a man-made structure. Material is added to the nest year after year until it becomes almost as conspicuous as the average bald-eagle nest. This osprey built on a foundation barely rising above the water's surface near Cowpens Key. Unlike the secretive woodcock, who steals cautiously to its nest, an osprey makes a dramatic arrival, beating its nearly six-foot wingspread and giving a wild, whistled call. Incubation, which lasts about a month, is shared by both parents.

Snowy egrets nest in colonies near water. In the southern United States they usually build their nests twelve feet or so up in trees and bushes, while on islands in Texas they often nest on opuntia cactus. This nest at the Bear River Migratory Bird Refuge in Utah is in a marsh. The egrets have mashed down vegetation, largely rushes, on which they have built a sparse platform just inches above the water.

Least bitterns, the smallest North American members of the heron family, rarely nest in a colony. They are shy and secretive, so they are often overlooked, although nearly all large freshwater marshes with sizable stands of reeds, cattails, and similar tall, sinuous plants have a few pairs during the nesting season. Bitterns often hide by holding their bills upright and "freezing" so that many people walk by without seeing them.

The Eggs Hatch

The bright pink skin of these day-old roseate spoonbills shows through their still-scant down. At this age the blunt mandibles show no indication of the spoon shape they will eventually acquire. The last egg of the clutch is pipped here, and the hatchling will soon join its siblings.

In the heron family both look-alike adults share nest duties. With its beautiful plumes lifted, this snowy egret returns to shelter the newly hatched young and continues to incubate the unhatched eggs. The tiny egret retains some of the nourishing yolk in its body and does not need to be fed immediately.

The least bittern is the only American species of heron whose sexes differ in color and are distinguishable in the field. As each egg hatches, the female picks up and discards the empty shell as a safety measure. The white lining of the shell as well as the odor of hatching could attract a predator if it were left in the nest.

Usually the bare skin around the bittern's bill is straw-yellow, but it will flame bright red from intense emotion when mates make their periodic exchange of nest duties. Reports of this blush by a few ornithologists were met with skepticism until Fred Truslow documented the fleeting color in this photograph.

These bitterns nest in a variety of freshwater marshes from the southern border of the United States to Canada. This bittern, sheltering four downy young and an unhatched egg, was photographed on July 1, 1963, on Howland's Island, New York.

Overleaf:
Many shorebirds habitually bob their tails, but of them all, the spotted sandpiper is the champion "teeter-tail." The sexes look alike but scientists have determined that the female does the courting and the male does most or all of the incubation of eggs. While this goes on, the female remains close by, and when the eggs hatch both parents care for the young. In contrast to young least bitterns, which stay in the nest for five days or more, these sandpipers leave as soon as they are dry. This hour-old chick with adult-sized feet climbs impatiently on the back of its parent, who continues to incubate the three unhatched eggs.

Sometimes an inexperienced parent either tries to feed its young before it is ready to accept food or offers food too large for the infant to swallow. This black skimmer was persistent in his attempt to feed a fish almost as large as the chick. Finally he gave up, ate the fish himself, and went off to catch a fish small enough for the infant to swallow.

Both sexes of this highly specialized species look alike, though the female is slightly smaller than the male, who usually stands guard as she incubates her four or five large, heavily spotted, and streaked eggs. Two eggs in this nest have hatched and the female continues to incubate the others while a one-hour-old baby crouches beside her. The male has temporarily left his guard post to round up the other infant, who wandered away from the nest.

A ruffed grouse broods her clutch of seven eggs. All grouse eggs hatch at almost the same time, and as soon as they are dry, the female leads her chicks away, leaving any unhatched eggs. She must protect the active chicks from predators even at the expense of late hatchlings.

More eggs appear to hatch in the morning than at any other time of the day or night. Here, one grouse chick was dry and ready to face the world at 6:15 A.M. Twenty minutes later, at 6:35, five young grouse were dry.

In the last photograph of this series, the female has already left the nest, and her chicks prepare to follow her. She leaves two unhatched eggs in the nest, to which she and her brood will never return.

The Growing Family

For twelve weeks in 1960 Fred Truslow kept an
almost daily vigil over the bald eagles on Murray
Key in Everglades National Park. From his lofty blind
thirty-three feet from the bulky nest, he recorded
with his camera the development and behavior of the
eagles. The downy eaglet beside the female is
twenty-one days old.

When the two eggs of the unique ground-nesting
barred owl hatched, the young were covered with
dense white down. This gradually darkened and
became mottled, blending into the surroundings. For
the first two weeks the female seldom left the nest
and the young were given food brought by the male.
Once during a huge rainstorm, when the nest was
swamped, Truslow's concern saved the family. He
moved the nest, chicks and all, to safety, returning it
to its place when the downpour was over.

Left: Young wood thrushes, like most members of the order *Passeriformes,* spend their early days sleeping and eating food placed in their bills by their parents. The way in which chicks of other orders are fed varies greatly. Grouse, for example, never put food in the mouths of their young; eagles and owls tear food apart and feed their very young offspring; gulls swallow the food they collect and regurgitate at the nest.

Both parents brought food at brief intervals for these ravenous young brown thrashers and stuffed it into their brightly colored mouths. At this stage the young birds ate almost their weight in food each day.

For a few days after hatching, the blind, naked, and helpless young cardinals are brooded by the female. The male collects the food, which the female accepts and gives to the young that beg most energetically. These cardinals were photographed in the Truslow back yard in Charlotte, North Carolina. Fred often advised beginning bird photographers that the back yard was a good place to start.

A cowbird sneaked into this prothonotary warbler nest and laid an egg. When hatched, the baby cowbird was larger and stronger than the baby warblers. The cowbird was so demanding that the parents, who averaged sixteen trips an hour to the nest with food, stuffed almost all of it into the gaping mouth of the young cowbird, who grew so fast it was soon larger than its foster parents, while the baby warblers starved.

Overleaf:
For the first two weeks or more, both mourning doves give their rapidly growing young "pigeon milk." This substance is secreted by the wall of their crop and is pumped into the open bill of the squab. This thirteen-day-old squab will soon have partly digested seeds added to its diet of milk. This nest was near an elementary school in Charlotte, where Fred enlisted the aid of one of the schoolchildren, who reported to him daily on the progress of the nest.

Both parents care for their young spoonbills. Unlike young herons, which seize the bill of the parent in a scissor grip when feeding, young spoonbills thrust their bill into the side of the adult's and reach into the throat for the partly digested minnows, prawns, and other tiny marine forms carried to the nest in the crop.

Still too weak to stand, this two-day-old spoonbill on Vingt-et-un Islands in Texas stretches along the parent's lower mandible as it reaches for sustenance.

As they grow and gain strength, the young spoonbills vie for first place at the food supply.

It is a fearsome sight to watch a ruby-throated hummingbird thrust her needle-sharp bill up and down as she pumps tiny insects and nectar into the receptive babies. But she never misjudges her target, though the young heads wave about wildly.

The nest becomes uncomfortably crowded as young birds approach fledging age. These restless young Baltimore orioles at Ithaca, New York, have climbed to the top of the socklike nest to await the arrival of a parent, this time the female, with food.

The Young Birds Fledge

Blue jays fledge between seventeen and twenty-one
days of age. Though their pattern and color are like
those of their look-alike parents, their very short tails
and colorful mouths opened wide as they beg for
food indicate their extreme youth. These five jays in
Summit, New Jersey, may fledge at any moment; if
one is pushed or falls from the nest, the others will
follow quickly. The nest was very close to the
entrance of the Truslow home and once, when a
party was scheduled, Fred put out a sign directing
guests to use the side door, lest they disturb his
birds.

The glossy black head, neck, and breast of a male
anhinga distinguish it from the female, who is
tawny-buff in those areas. These juveniles, almost
ready to fledge, look more like the female than the
male. They often spar in the nest, which sometimes
leads to disgorged food, foreshadowing adult
behavior.

Almost two months old, these rough-legged hawks, swiveling their necks to watch a parent with food circling overhead, are almost ready to fledge from their nest of sagebrush in southern Montana. They are cosmopolitan birds, occurring also in Scandinavia, Russia, and Siberia. Probably no hawk in the world is a more valuable catcher of rodents than this species. Though Fred Truslow photographed dozens of species, from grebes to sparrows, he most enjoyed photographing birds of the order *Falconiformes* because they presented the greatest challenge to his skill, knowledge, patience, and alertness. These hawks are completely unaware of the photographer's presence in his nearby blind.

(A) On January 15, 1960, two pale downy eagles on Murray Key in Florida Bay were fourteen days old. The female rarely left them after they broke out of their eggs but sheltered them from the hot sun and nighttime cold, while food was brought to the nest by the male. (B) By the time they were twenty-one days old, the young eagles' natal down was largely replaced by a woolly, blackish covering. The male brought little but fish to his family. From these the female tore tidbits and placed them in the open mouths of the weak youngsters. (C) Now twenty-five days old, the ravenous eaglets are fed in turn by the female. Not until they were more than three weeks old did she permit the male to feed them. Unlike the female, he did this by stuffing food into one eaglet until it could swallow no more; only then did he give food to the second eaglet. (D) The hooded yellow eyes of the parents inspect their young, whose eyes remain dark until they approach maturity some time in their third year. They may not acquire full adult plumage until they are four to six years old. (E) At thirty-two days, the young eagles are no longer passive but move freely about the nest. Not yet in control of their bodies, they often fall flat, but sometimes they will use their wings as if they were feet and walk about on all fours. (F) It was a very hot day when Fred made this photograph. The young eagles are resting after their exercise and growing activities. They, like other birds, have no sweat glands in their skin. Instead, air sacs in their bodies collect warm moist air from overheated tissues and, with their mouths wide open, the eagles expel excessive heat as they increase their rate of breathing. (G) At fifty-one days, the heavy wings can be spread but muscles are not yet strong enough to lift them. To fold the extended wings, the eagle has to sidle first one way and then another, letting them collapse with their own weight. Down still reaches almost to the toes but will soon wear away, leaving the tarsus bare. (H) It is February 28 and the eagles, nearly two months old, exercise vigorously. They clinch their talons in a tremendous effort, and their strengthening wings lift them a few feet above the nest. (I) Feathers are well developed and wings are lifted strongly by the time the eaglets are sixty-seven days old.

A

D

G

B

C

E

F

H

I

Now in late March the young eagles are eighty-three days old and almost ready to make their first flight. In twelve weeks they have grown from three to thirty-six inches in length. Fed by hard-working parents, they are heavier than they will be a few weeks hence, after they have begun the strenuous life of flying and caring for themselves.

Except for some speckles on their plumage, young fledgling swallow-tailed kites look like their parents. In a few more days these two young kites will skim gracefully over the grassy meadows of Everglades National Park with sufficient speed to catch swift-flying dragonflies, a favorite food of this species.

When young roseate spoonbills are seven or eight weeks old, they begin practice flights. They gather with their peers along the shore, where they bathe, learn to find food, and try to perfect their flying skills. They continue to mob the adults, begging for food, long after they are able to care for themselves. At this stage their heads are still feathered and only a delicate pink flush on parts of their white plumage foreshadows the bright colors they will wear as adults.

The Time of Parting

Overleaf:
As summer advances, the diligently reared young birds have finally fledged and have severed the ties with nest and parent. A new generation of birds is in the air, ready to follow the habits and paths of its ancestors. In time each will repeat the nesting cycle in a manner inherited from its forebears. Here, white pelicans circle high above their nesting island in Great Salt Lake, Utah, as they begin their flight toward winter quarters on the Salton Sea and other southern waters.

Looking Back: An Afterword by Mildred MacCutcheon Truslow

Frederick Kent Truslow was born in 1902 and grew up in Summit, New Jersey. In those early years so long ago, Summit was a country town and Fred's home was surrounded by fields and thick woods. Each day before school he was up early, roaming the countryside and watching birds for hours at a time, while keeping careful notes of his observations.

At the age of thirteen Fred wrote an essay about the slaughter of beautiful Everglades egrets for their plumage, for which he won first prize in an Audubon contest. It was printed in the local paper, and he was honored with a luncheon at the American Museum of Natural History in New York City with the great ornithologist Dr. Frank M. Chapman.

In later years he almost forgot his days in the field, as he entered the business world. During World War II, he was told that he was too old for active service, so he joined a large company involved in war work; he was made Director of Protection for all their plants, later manager of their largest plant. In Summit, he served on the City Council for nine years and was appointed Commissioner of Police. He was an expert shot and taught revolver shooting during the war years. He had so many talents that he was kept very busy.

Fate must have sent Allan Cruickshank, the famous Audubon lecturer and photographer, to Summit in 1951, for, although Allan didn't know it then, he was to become a major influence in Fred's life. When he showed his beautiful wildlife films, I knew that Fred would love to do the same thing—it would deeply touch his interest in birds, his love of the outdoors, and his knowledge of the camera. But he was too busy and overworked to think of leaving his jobs.

In 1956, however, Fred was utterly exhausted, and his doctor decreed complete rest. It was then that I remembered Allan's lecture and felt that Fred's health would be restored if he could spend some time in the open. We bought a station wagon and drove to Florida, heading for Everglades National Park. On our way, we stopped to see Allan Cruickshank and his wife, Helen, also a well-known writer and photographer. They were very kind and suggested camera equipment, recommending that Fred start taking pictures on the Anhinga Trail in the park. En route to Miami, he kept insisting that his Brownie camera and three rolls of film were more than enough, but I finally persuaded him to enter a camera shop. Four hours later he emerged, beaming and carrying several large packages.

The next few weeks were full of excitement. Fred's old interest in birds had returned, and he was up early each morning to take photographs and learn about the workings of his new equipment. We were near Everglades National Park, where abundant wildlife attracted many scientists. Fred soon met Daniel Beard, the Park Superintendent, and Dr. William Robertson, Park Biologist. District Rangers Clifford Senne, Erwin Winte, and Ernest Borgman also were a great help through the years. Robert Porter Allen, Research Director for the Audubon Society, distinguished for his studies of endangered species, became his good friend, and later they would collaborate on three articles for the *National Geographic* magazine.

Fred was happy and rested now, and his health had improved considerably. He decided not to return to New York, but to devote his life to recording the behavior and beauty of birds.

In 1957, friends suggested that Fred show his pictures to the *National Geographic* editorial staff. So, on our way back to New Jersey for the summer, we stopped in Washington. When the people at *National Geographic* saw his photography, they asked for an article. Shortly thereafter, "Limpkin, the Crying Bird That

Haunts Florida Swamps" was published. This was to be the first of twelve articles in the magazine which would feature his pictures. Edwin (Buddy) Wisherd, head of their photographic laboratories, saw great promise in Fred's work and later became one of his closest friends. Buddy stressed the importance of using the right film: one with a minimum of grain and with well-balanced color which would produce crisp, sharp images. He also recommended the lenses that Fred would use the rest of his life. He would learn to operate them almost instinctively, freeing his attention to concentrate on the subjects' behavior and the composition of the photograph.

Fred used two 35 mm camera bodies, one with a motor drive. His standard lenses were a 200 mm for hand-held and flight shots and a 400 mm which he used for ninety percent of his work. Later on he added an 80-200 mm zoom lens, which was useful when working close to a nest. He always felt it was better to have one really topnotch lens than a dozen of lesser quality, and so he obtained the finest available at that time. A sturdy, quickly adjustable tripod and easily portable strobe lights were also essential. Generally speaking, he kept his equipment as simple as possible.

He almost always worked from a blind, using a Pop-Tent that operated on an umbrella principle, with extra zippers for ventilation. He felt that camouflage was not necessary, as birds will see the blind no matter what is done, but if it blends into the surroundings, people may not see it. One unwanted visitor investigating can ruin a whole day of photography. On the other hand, a "walk-away" partner can make things easier. When he leaves, the birds will think everyone has gone. Fred found that movement alarms birds but stationary objects do not seem to bother them. However, it may take some time before they will accept a new blind near the nest.

Fred took great care not to disturb nesting birds. When he started to photograph the eagles on Murray Key, he built a complete tower for his blind in our back yard in Homestead. After it was finished, he drove fifty miles to Flamingo with the whole framework tied to the top of the station wagon, then boated it the rest of the way. When both adult birds had left the nest, the twenty-foot tower was erected with the blind already in place, thanks to the help of Ernest Borgman, Bruce Shaw, and Jim Arnott. Then he watched all day to be sure that the birds would accept it. If they had shown any signs of deserting the nest, he would have given up the project.

He felt that no one should ever consider bird photography without having a genuine concern for the protection of the subjects. He must learn how birds behave, take time to really study them, and even note that individuals of the same species do not always behave in the same way. This knowledge is best learned by much experience in the field and close observation.

Although Fred always had a camera with him, he never began working until he was well acquainted with the birds' actions. He needed to know how often they came to the nest, where they perched, what they did before leaving to feed, and how close he could come without alarming them. Then he would be ready to place his blind quickly in the right position and to anticipate the actions he hoped to photograph. This was followed by many hours, days, and sometimes weeks in the blind. Endless patience was required as he waited. Sometimes he was rewarded with the unexpected, but the welfare of the birds was his first concern; it was more important than the most perfect photograph of the species.

Many people asked him what kind of camera he used. They thought if they could obtain the same kind they would achieve the same beautiful pictures. But it was not the special camera or lens. It was Fred's devotion to his task, his built-in sense of composition and timing, and his tremendous patience and perseverance.

Bird photography, done with care, is exhausting. Fred spent thirteen and a half weeks watching the bald eagles, often nine hours a day, in a mosquito-filled blind. To photograph golden eagles in Montana, he worked from a blind on a ledge overhanging a four-hundred-and-fifty-foot drop straight into the valley below. Also in Montana, when he was working on the rare trumpeter swans, icy lake water rose up to his waist; on one occasion he was so paralyzed by the cold that he had to call for help on his CB radio. Once while photographing on Florida Bay, sitting for many hours in a small blind, he became so numb that he couldn't move. It would have been disastrous if Park Ranger "Whitey" had not come in the nick of time to rescue him. Fred once passed out from heat exhaustion photographing the California condors, and when he was working with whooping cranes in Texas a deadly four-and-a-half-foot cottonmouth snake crawled into his blind. Ever so slowly he moved one leg of his tripod and used it to urge the snake gently to leave the blind.

Fred never photographed a captive bird. He insisted that they be free and wild, able to come and go. He wanted natural, clear, and understandable portraits. In this most difficult photography, he was able to achieve his greatest wish, to record the birds' true behavior, often caught in a split second. His skill enriched the knowledge of ornithologists, and several of the pictures he obtained showed patterns of behavior that had not been known to science.

In 1958 Fred met Dr. Arthur A. Allen, the world-famous ornithologist at Cornell University. He and his family became our good friends, and we saw them often. Dr. Allen was a great help, and so was his son, David, whom Fred described as "a fine wildlife photographer and one of the most knowledgeable men in his field."

Fred thrived on his new career. He traveled to the four corners of the United States to photograph birds. He was helped by many wonderful people, made new friends, and in turn helped many others. Over the years, his major photographic essays appeared in *National Geographic* and many of his pictures were used in their books *Song and Garden Birds* and *Water, Prey and Game Birds.* His photographs graced the covers or pages of *Audubon Magazine* and *National Wildlife.* He also contributed to *The Living Bird,* an annual publication of Cornell's Laboratory of Ornithology, of whose board of directors he became a member.

Others, too, recognized Fred's skill. When President Lyndon Johnson wanted an eagle picture for his book *No Retreat from Tomorrow,* he chose one of Fred's photographs. The National Geographic Society awarded its prestigious Hubbard medal to Neil Armstrong, Edwin Aldrin, and Michael Collins for man's first landing on the moon in the module "Eagle." At the ceremony, the president of the society presented each of them with an enlargement of one of Fred's pictures of an eagle landing. An autographed photograph of the occasion was sent to Fred and still hangs in his study.

When he became so very ill, it was sad to see him put away his "tools," never again to photograph the beauties of nature. His ideas, knowledge, and techniques have been passed on to a new generation of photographers. In years to come there will be many technical advances, but the perfection of Fred's work will still cause amazement and the pictures he achieved will be his greatest memorial.

EDITOR'S NOTE: On August 19, 1978, Frederick Kent Truslow died at the age of seventy-five.

Notes on the Photographs

PAGE

1. Eggs of the Arctic Tern   (*Sterna paradisaea*)
   Machias Seal Island, Maine: 1958
   50mm lens at 1/50 and *f*:8

2. Great Egret   (*Casmerodius albus*)
   Vingt-et-un Islands, Texas: 1960
   300mm lens at 1/125 and *f*:8

4. Cedar Waxwing   (*Bombycilla cedrorum*)
   Ithaca, New York: 1960
   300mm lens at 1/2000 and *f*:16

6–7. Black Skimmer   (*Rynchops niger*)
   Coot Bay, Florida: 1969
   200mm lens at 1/500 and *f*:6.5

8. Osprey   (*Pandion haliaetus*)
   Florida Bay, Florida: 1958
   400mm lens at 1/125 and *f*:6.5

65. Great Blue Heron   (*Ardea herodias*)
   Vingt-et-un Islands, Texas: 1960
   300mm lens at 1/125 and *f*:8

66–7. Mixed waders including Great Egret (*Casmerodius albus*), Snowy Egret (*Egretta thula*), Roseate Spoonbill (*Ajaia ajaja*), White Ibis (*Eudocimus albus*), and Wood Stork (*Mycteria americana*)
   Everglades National Park, Florida: 1973
   58mm lens at 1/125 and *f*:6.5

68. Western Grebe   (*Aechmophorus occidentalis*)
   Bear River Migratory Bird Refuge, Utah: 1959
   400mm lens at 1/125 and *f*:6.5

68. California Gull   (*Larus californicus*)
   Bear River Migratory Bird Refuge, Utah: 1959
   400mm lens at 1/125 and *f*:6.5

69. Common Gallinule   (*Gallinula chloropus*)
   Everglades National Park, Florida: 1963
   400mm lens at 1/125 and *f*:6.5

70–1. Gannet   (*Morus bassanus*)
   Bonaventure Island, Quebec: 1958
   Fighting sequence: 400mm lens at 1/100 and *f*:6.5
   Close-up of heads: 400mm lens at 1/125 and *f*:8
   Long view: 50mm lens at 1/125 and *f*:11

72–3. Wood Stork   (*Mycteria americana*)
   Aerial view: Cuthbert Rookery, Florida: 1959
   90mm lens at 1/500 and *f*:2.8
   Close-up: East River Rookery, Florida: 1963
   400mm lens at 1/125 and *f*:10

74–5. Yellow-shafted (Common) Flicker   (*Colaptes auratus*)
   Homestead, Florida: 1962
   400mm lens at 1/125 and *f*:7

76–7. Bald Eagle   (*Haliaeetus leucocephalus*)
   Murray Key, Florida: 1960
   400mm lens at 1/125 and *f*:6.5

78. Eggs of the Black Skimmer   (*Rynchops niger*)
   Great Egg Harbor, New Jersey: 1958
   50mm lens at 1/125 and *f*:11

79. Eggs of the Common Puffin   (*Fratercula arctica*)
   Machias Seal Island, Maine: 1957
   50mm lens at 1/125 and *f*:5.6

80–1. Pileated Woodpecker   (*Dryocopus pileatus*)
   Everglades National Park, Florida: 1966
   400mm lens at 1/125 and *f*:7

82. American Avocet   (*Recurvirostra americana*)
   Bear River Migratory Bird Refuge, Utah: 1959
   400mm lens at 1/125 and *f*:6.5

83. Black-necked Stilt   (*Himantopus mexicanus*)
   Bear River Migratory Bird Refuge, Utah: 1959
   400mm lens at 1/125 and *f*:6.5

84. Barred Owl   (*Strix varia*)
   Everglades National Park, Florida: 1963
   400mm lens at 1/60 and *f*:16

85. Everglade Kite   (*Rostrhamus sociabilis*)
   Lake Okeechobee, Florida: 1963
   400mm lens at 1/125 and *f*:6.5

86. Eastern Kingbird   (*Tyrannus tyrannus*)
   Ithaca, New York: 1963
   300mm lens at 1/2000 and *f*:16

87. Prothonotary Warbler   (*Protonotaria citrea*)
   Wadesboro, North Carolina: 1972
   300mm lens at 1/2000 and *f*:18

88–9. American Woodcock   (*Philohela minor*)
Ithaca, New York: 1975
400mm lens at 1/60 and *f*:6.5

90–1. Osprey   (*Pandion haliaetus*)
Cowpens Key, Florida: 1963
200mm at 1/500 and *f*:5.6

92. Snowy Egret   (*Egretta thula*)
Bear River Migratory Bird Refuge, Utah: 1959
400mm lens at 1/125 and *f*:8

93. Least Bittern   (*Ixobrychus exilis*)
Howland's Island, New York: 1963
400mm lens at 1/2500 and *f*:25

94. Roseate Spoonbill   (*Ajaia ajaja*)
Vingt-et-un Islands, Texas: 1969
90mm lens at 1/50 and *f*:5

95. Snowy Egret   (*Egretta thula*)
Bear River Migratory Bird Refuge, Utah: 1959
400mm lens at 1/125 and *f*:8

96–7. Least Bittern   (*Ixobrychus exilis*)
Howland's Island, New York: 1963
400mm lens at 1/2500 and *f*:25

98–9. Spotted Sandpiper   (*Actitis macularia*)
Ithaca, New York: 1963
400mm lens at 1/2000 and *f*:20

100–1. Black Skimmer   (*Rynchops niger*)
Great Egg Harbor, New Jersey: 1958
400mm lens at 1/125 and *f*:6.5

102–3. Ruffed Grouse   (*Bonasa umbellus*)
Enfield, New York: 1961
Brooding: 300mm lens at 1/2000 and *f*:16
Young: 400mm lens at 1/50 and *f*:12

104. Bald Eagle   (*Haliaeetus leucocephalus*)
Murray Key, Florida: 1960
400mm lens at 1/125 and *f*:6.5

105. Barred Owl   (*Strix varia*)
Everglades National Park, Florida: 1963
400mm lens at 1/60 and *f*:14

106. Wood Thrush   (*Hylocichla mustelina*)
Ithaca, New York: 1961
400mm lens at 1/2000 at *f*:16

107. Brown Thrasher   (*Toxostema rufum*)
Charlotte, North Carolina: 1973
200mm lens at 1/2000 and *f*:18

108. Cardinal   (*Cardinalis cardinalis*)
Charlotte, North Carolina: 1972
400mm lens at 1/2000 and *f*:18

109. Prothonotary Warbler   (*Protonotaria citrea*)
Wadesboro, North Carolina: 1972
300mm lens at 1/2000 and *f*:18

110–11. Mourning Doves   (*Zenaida macroura*)
Charlotte, North Carolina: 1973
400mm lens at 1/2000 and *f*:18

112–13. Roseate Spoonbill   (*Ajaia ajaja*)
Vingt-et-un Islands, Texas: 1960
Family portrait: 300mm lens at 1/125 and *f*:7
Feeding shots: 400mm lens at 1/125 and *f*:7

114. Ruby-throated Hummingbird   (*Archilochus colubris*)
Ithaca, New York: 1961
400mm lens at 1/2000 and *f*:14

115. Baltimore (Northern) Oriole   (*Icterus galbula*)
Ithaca, New York: 1961
300mm lens at 1/2000 and *f*:16

116. Blue Jay   (*Cyanocitta cristata*)
Summit, New Jersey: 1957
300mm lens at 1/1000 and *f*:9.5

117. Anhinga   (*Anhinga anhinga*)
Everglades National Park, Florida: 1963
400mm lens at 1/125 and *f*:6.5

118–19. Rough-legged Hawks   (*Buteo lagopus*)
Wilsall, Montana: 1964
58mm at 1/125 and *f*:14

120–22. Bald Eagle (*Haliaeetus leucocephalus*)
Murray Key, Florida: 1960
A–G: 400mm lens at 1/125 and *f*:6.5
H, I: 400mm lens at 1/250 and *f*:4
Fledglings: 90mm lens at 1/125 and *f*:5.6

123. Swallow-tailed Kite (*Elanoides forficatus*)
Everglades National Park, Florida: 1970
400mm lens at 1/125 and *f*:6.5

124–25. Roseate Spoonbill (*Ajaia ajaja*)
Cowpens Key, Florida: 1958
400mm lens at 1/100 and *f*:6.5

126–27. American White Pelicans (*Pelecanus erythrorhynchos*)
Great Salt Lake, Utah: 1959
90mm lens at 1/500 and *f*:2.8

128. Bald Eagle (*Haliaeetus leucocephalus*)
Big Bob Key, Florida: 1969
400mm at 1/500 and *f*:5

Fred Truslow used standard 35 mm. cameras with motor drive and an assortment of lenses. All of these photographs were made with Kodachrome film.